D1250478

ON

GURDJIEFF

Garrett Thomson
The College of Wooster

THOMSON

WADSWORTH

Australia • Canada • Mexico • Singapore • Spain • United Kingdom • United States

COPYRIGHT © 2003 Wadsworth,
a division of Thomson Learning, Inc.
Thomson Learning™ is a trademark
used herein under license.

ALL RIGHTS RESERVED. No part of
this work covered by the copyright
hereon, may be reproduced or used in
any form or by any means—graphic,
electronic, or mechanical, including,
but not limited to, photocopying,
recording, taping, Web distribution,
information networks, or information
storage and retrieval systems—without
the written permission of the publisher.

Printed in the United States of America.

1 2 3 4 5 6 7 06 05 04 03 02

0-534-58390-3

**For more information about our
products, contact us at:
Thomson Learning Academic
Resource Center
1-800-423-0563**

**For permission to use material from
this text, contact us by:
Phone: 1-800-730-2214
Fax: 1-800-731-2215
Web: www.thomsonrights.com**

Asia
Thomson Learning
5 Shenton Way #01-01
UIC Building
Singapore 068808

Australia
Nelson Thomson Learning
102 Dodds Street
South Street
South Melbourne, Victoria 3205
Australia

Canada
Nelson Thomson Learning
1120 Birchmount Road
Toronto, Ontario M1K 5G4
Canada

Europe/Middle East/South Africa
Thomson Learning
High Holborn House
50-51 Bedford Row
London WC1R 4LR
United Kingdom

Latin America
Thomson Learning
Seneca, 53
Colonia Polanco
11560 Mexico D.F.
Mexico

Spain
Paraninfo Thomson Learning
Calle/Magallanes, 25
28015 Madrid, Spain

CONTENTS

Preface

Gurdjieff presents us with an unusual way of understanding the human condition. His system is not part of the Judaic-Christian-Islamic, nor the Buddhist and Hindu, mainstream traditions. Although it contains elements from these religions, Gurdjieff's system as a whole is quite different from them. It includes a concoction of Sufi, Tibetan, Zoroastrian, Pythagorean, and Gnostic influences.

Another striking feature of Gurdjieff's teaching is that it is very single-minded. Almost all of his teaching is directed towards explaining how humans need to and can practice self-transformation.

Gurdjieff's ideas have had an impact on influential writers and persons of the twentieth century such as Katherine Mansfield, Aldous Huxley, J.B. Priestly, Henry Miller, Fritz Schumaker, Frank Lloyd Wright, Jean Toomer, and possibly T.S.Eliot.

Gurdjieff is not a philosopher in the academic sense of the term. He does not advance arguments for clearly defined positions. He does not distinguish conceptual and empirical claims, or systematically explain the key words and analogies in his system. Typically, he and his followers do not defend their claims against objections. For example, many of his cosmological claims contradict contemporary science. These limitations mean that Gurdjieff is not an academic philosopher, although of course he never pretends to be and would scorn the academic discipline as worthless in terms of the human task of self-transformation.

Nevertheless, Gurdjieff is a lover of wisdom. Since the traditional definition of 'philosophy,' based on its etymology, is the love of wisdom, Gurdjieff does qualify as a philosopher in this sense. He presents a powerful view of the human condition.

The aim of this book is to introduce the basic teachings of Gurdjieff to the general reader. In the first chapter, I explain Gurdjieff's description of the human condition, the state of incompleteness most of us are in. Chapters 2 and 3 will explain how we can evolve out of that state. In Chapters 4 and 5, I shall explain these ideas in relation to Gurdjieff's cosmology and metaphysics. Finally I examine their implications for our normal understanding of morality, religion, epistemology and science (in Chapters 6, 7, 8 and 9).

Towards the end of the book, I try to give a general evaluation of some aspects of Gurdjieff's system. Otherwise, I have tried to merely report succinctly and faithfully in an organized and clear fashion. At key points, I have compared Gurdjieff's views to philosophers of the past, such as Hume and Nietzsche. This book contains a bibliography, a biography and also a brief glossary of special terms used by Gurdjieff.

Obviously, this work is made possible by the many other writings on Gurdjieff. I am heavily indebted to the books of Ouspensky, Bennett, and, of course, the writings of Gurdjieff himself. Chapter 10 is indebted to the biography written by Moore.

For the sake of brevity, I have used abbreviations for some references. 'Bel' for Gurdjieff's book *Beelzebub's Tales to his Grandson*. 'MRM' stands for *Meetings with Remarkable Men*, and 'TS' for the *Third Series* or *Life is Real Only Then, When "I Am."* 'SM' stands for Ouspensky's work *In Search of the Miraculous* and 'FW' for his *The Fourth Way*. Maurice Nicoll's *Psychological Commentaries on the Teaching of Gurdjieff and Ouspensky* will be abbreviated with 'N,' with a number that indicates the relevant volume of the five-volume work.

Thank you to Prof. Dan Kolak for encouraging me to write this book and for his very helpful suggestions. I would like to dedicate this work to my friend Muchtar Martins.

1
A Psychology of Everyday Life

The core of Gurdjieff's teaching is that we humans are radically incomplete beings who need to transform ourselves. Most of the time, we live on automatic pilot and are barely conscious. We are asleep. More radically, we really do not exist as persons at all. We are machines. Nevertheless, we can become whole by surmounting our mechanical nature and acquiring a will. By waking from our sleeping state, we can become fully conscious. Furthermore, in this way, we can fulfill our role in the grand cosmological system. The universe consists of different and interconnected concentrations of energy, which flow out from and back to the Absolute. As they flow out, these emanations of energy become denser in discrete steps that constitute different levels of being. As they return to the Absolute, they become finer and, by becoming fully conscious, we participate in this evolutionary process.

Gurdjieff's ideas are complimented by a variety of practical exercises, which he learned during his voyages throughout Asia as a young adult (1887-1907). These practices formed part of his teaching, which is perhaps best known through the writings of the Russian intellectual Ouspensky, especially *In Search of the Miraculous* and *The Fourth Way*. However, we should set our explanation of these teachings in the context of Gurdjieff's own book, *Beelzebub's Tales to his Grandson*, which he completed in 1928. It is the first volume of a three part series called *All and Everything* and it is dedicated to destroying people's false beliefs about reality and themselves. It is from

3

Beelzebub's point of view that we should describe the psychology of our everyday condition.

Beelzebub's Tales

Beelzebub, now old and wise, was originally from the planet Karatas, near the center of the universe. In his fiery and immature youth, he organized a rebellion against His Endlessness and was banished, with his followers, to a remote solar system, Ors, to the planet Mars. He was forced to live in conditions of hardship, which were contrary to his nature (Bel, p.52-3). During his prolonged stay on Mars, Beelzebub visited the earth six times and was able to study the human condition. Due to the intervention of Ashiata Shiemash, a holy messenger himself sent to the earth, Beelzebub now has been pardoned and has been allowed to return to Karatas (Bel, p.54).

At the beginning of Gurdjieff's book, Beelzebub is traveling on the ship Karnak, with his attendants, including his servant Ahoon, and his grandson Hassein, from Karatas to another solar system, in order to attend a conference on the planet Revozvradendr, regarding some events of great importance that require his wisdom. Hassein is a young adolescent, equivalent in years to a 12-year-old human. Beelzebub decides to educate his grandson by telling him tales of his exile (Bel, p.129). The ship Karnak has been delayed by the passing of a comet (Bel, p.56). Most of Gurdjieff's book consists in the tales of Beelzebub's time in exile, told while the ship is waiting for the comet and its dangerous gases to pass.

Towards the end of the book, Beelzebub also narrates what happens after the two-month stay on Revozvradendr on the return journey to Karatas. It consists of more tales and an important description of a visit to the Holy Planet Purgatory, where Beelzebub went to greet friends and family, including his son, Tooilan.

Afterwards, while the ship is in transit, various archangels and angels visit the ship Karnak to restore Beelzebub's horns, which were taken from him at the time of his exile. This ceremony creates much anticipation because the number of forks that appear on Beelzebub's horns will reveal the degree of objective Reason he has attained. As the horns spout, everyone is astonished to see that Beelzebub's horns have five forks, which means that he has reached the highest level of Reason that any being can attain (Bel, p.1177). Beelzebub, who is a three-brained being like us humans, has attained this level through his own 'conscious labors and intentional sufferings.' Hassein is overcome with a feeling of humility, and as a result, he acquires a feeling of deep love for the three-brained beings of earth. Beelzebub permits his grandson one last question before they land on Karatas, and Hassein asks what can be done to save the people of earth. Beelzebub replies that the only way of saving them would be if they could constantly sense the inevitability of their own deaths and that of those persons that they meet (Bel, p. 1183).

Beelzebub is sufficient similar to us humans that we can learn from his experiences of earth and from the example of his own self-development. At the same time, he is sufficiently dissimilar to us that his descriptions of human life and psychology strike us as alien. They are told from a distant point of view. This distance has two implications. First, being distant, Beelzebub's descriptions are removed from the pettiness of our lives. Second, despite the fact that Beelzebub has to simplify his descriptions of humans for the sake of his grandson, they are alien to the ordinary reader who has to make a special effort to understand them. In particular, Beelzebub's tales are full of allegories, and one is never certain which aspects of the work are allegorical and which are literal. Remember that the book is the first in a trilogy and is intended to destroy our preconceptions about reality and ourselves. Although many aspects of Gurdjieff's thought are explained by Ouspensky's reports of Gurdjieff's early talks, the perspective from which we may best view this teaching is Beelzebub's.

Human beings are radically incomplete. Gurdjieff expresses this point with two analogies. We have within us a large mansion with many beautiful rooms, but we are locked in the basement and kitchen, unable to use our full potential (FW, p.2). We humans live in a small part of ourselves (SM, p.145). The second analogy extends the first. A human being is like a house, full of servants with no master. Each servant tries to do the work of the other and the result is chaos. In other words, we lack a will or master, who can assign the servants their proper work (FW, p.33).

The underdeveloped condition we should want to escape from is marked by two main characteristics: being asleep and being mechanical, which respectively describe our level of consciousness and our lack of will. These two central ideas can be best explained by examining five features of our everyday state, which are:

    a) Being asleep,
    b) Fragmentation of the self,
    c) Being mechanical,
    d) Lack of will, and
    e) Self-deception.

a) Being Asleep

According to Gurdjieff, sleep is the chief feature of our being. It is possible to live a whole life in a hypnotic trance or a state of sleep. The idea that we humans normally live in a state of sleep is an old one, reminiscent of Plato's (427-347 BC) famous analogy of the cave.

Of course, this idea of waking sleep is an analogy and, cashed out, Gurdjieff's claim is that humans are capable of four distinct states of consciousness, which Gurdjieff characterizes as different degrees of Reason in his first book (Bel. p. 770). The first state is that of being asleep literally, as we are at night. The second is everyday normal consciousness, which Gurdjieff also calls being asleep. The third Gurdjieff calls self-consciousness, a state that we can only have glimpses of after a long period of work on oneself, through the art of remembering oneself. The fourth state of consciousness is called 'objective consciousness,' and it can only be reached by passing through the third state (FW, p.5). We shall describe these states of consciousness in more detail in the next chapter.

What evidence does Gurdjieff give for the claim that we are normally asleep? First, it is incredibly difficult to remember oneself except for very brief stretches of time. Remembering oneself, which is described in more detail in Chapter 3, consists in being aware that one is. Such awareness usually only lasts for a few moments and we quickly forget ourselves as we identify ourselves with what we attend to and lose ourselves in our activities. According to Gurdjieff, this inability to remember oneself permanently shows that we are in a state of hypnotic sleep.

Second, in explaining what our being asleep means, Gurdjieff often appeals to the other features of our everyday existence, such as the fragmentation of ourselves, our mechanical way of living, self-deception and our attachment to and identification with negative feelings, all of which will be described later. In particular, our sleeping state is characterized by the fact we identify ourselves with our thoughts and feelings. This means that we cannot separate ourselves from those states, and this sends us to sleep.

Third, being in waking sleep is characterized by dreaming and automatic action. In this state of sleep, we mix imagination, illusions, and fantasy with awareness of reality. For instance, one imagines something and then forgets that it was imagined (FW, p.7). For example, we imagine unpleasant things that might happen to us. In brief, when we are asleep, we daydream.

Fourth, in the final analysis, to be really convinced that one is asleep, it is necessary to try to awaken and taste the third level of consciousness. One might say that all the other forms of evidence that one is asleep are merely circumstantial, and that the real evidence comes from waking up.

b) The Fragmentation of the Self

Another characteristic of our human condition is our absence of unity. Each of us falsely imagines that he or she is a single person (Gurdjieff, 1975, p75). Gurdjieff says:

> We suppose that we refer to the same thing all the time when we use the term 'I.' In reality, we are divided in hundreds of different 'I's (FW, p.4).

Gurdjieff's claim that there is no single 'I' has three aspects. First, he is denying the existence of a real self. This includes, but is not limited to, the denial of an underlying, non-material and immortal soul of the kind argued for by, for example, Descartes (1596–1650) in the Christian tradition. However, Gurdjieff's claim involves more than this metaphysical statement. The point is that we lack a self. Because it is possible for us to acquire a self, and thereby a soul (of a kind), Gurdjieff's claim is that we do not exist at all, except as a collection of automatic reactions.

Second, our current state is similar to a person with split and contradictory personalities, but who identifies with each of them. For example, one takes a decision but does not act on it, because the self who decides is different from the one who has to carry out the decision. This also explains why it is sometimes so difficult to keep one's promises; the self that makes the promise may be different from the one that has to keep it. In a similar vein, our likes and dislikes change according to external circumstances, and we behave very differently according to our roles and outside conditions. A person behaves, thinks and feels in one way at home, and in quite another way at work with his superiors, and in another with his or her subordinates. The person reacts in yet another way with his or her friends, and so on (FW, p.33). Outside of these repertoires or roles, the person feels very uncomfortable and tries his or her best to return to one of them (SM, p.240). In other words, we consist of different psychological compartments, and we live in them one at a time, identifying with them, usually unaware of the contradictions between them (FW, p.252). In this sense, we lack unity.

7

Third, Gurdjieff affirms, 'Every mood, thought, and sensation says 'I'' (SM, p. 59). The idea is that we identify ourselves with these different states, moods, and aspects of our personalities. We say 'I' to all of them, thereby making self-observation impossible (N1, p.59). According to Gurdjieff, humans constantly identify themselves with what attracts their attention (SM, p.150). For example, persons may identify themselves with a small problem in front of them and completely forget the great aims with which they began their work. 'Two or three trees nearest to them represent the whole wood' (SM, p.150). As a result, a person becomes like a mere thing (SM, p.150). By identifying in this way, we lose the capacity to remember ourselves. We send ourselves to sleep.

These different selves, or personalities, can co-exist, despite the contradictions between them, because, involuntarily, we have created buffers which protect us from noticing these contradictions (FW, p.34). These automatic responses are part of our being asleep, and an important aspect of the Gurdjieffian work consists in destroying buffers that permit us to lie to ourselves. Furthermore, these selves can be arranged in groupings that have been created by education or by a religion. Strong selves can dominate groups of weaker ones.

What does all this mean? Clearly, there is some sense in which one is a single person. For example, one could not escape repaying a bank loan on the grounds that one was a different person when one took out the loan. Ouspensky expresses this point by claiming that the whole person exists only as a physical thing or as an abstract concept.

Furthermore, to clarify Gurdjieff's claim, one might differentiate the subject or the 'I' from the 'me' or the selves that constitute our personality (Bennett, 1964, p.41). The 'I' is the featureless subject of any experience. Kant calls this the Transcendental Unity of Apperception (Thomson, 2000, p.12). It is the pure knower or subject that can never be the object of any experience. On the other hand, the 'me' consists in the different selves, moods and feelings that comprise our fragmented personality. Such a distinction is implicit in Gurdjieff's claim that we identify ourselves with our moods and feelings. The 'I' that identifies itself must be distinct from the feelings and personalities that it falsely identifies itself with. The 'I' that lives in the different compartments is not identical to those compartments. In other words, the subject (the 'I') is not the same as the multitude of selves (the 'me'), with which it often identifies itself.

Comparison with Hume

The Scottish philosopher David Hume (1711–1776) argued against the idea of a permanent soul substance and self on the grounds that all concepts must be derived from sensory experience and that there can be no experience of the self. There can be no experience of such a self because the self is the subject having the experience rather than being the object of any experience. Consequently, argues Hume, there can be no concept of the self.

There seem to be some similarities between Gurdjieff's view and Hume's. For instance, given Hume's position, it would be more accurate to say 'It thinks' and 'There is thought' rather than 'I think.' Compare this with Ouspensky's report of Gurdjieff's claim: 'With you: it observes, just as it speaks... You do not feel: I observe, I see... Everything is noticed, or seen, or thought (SM, p.117-118).

However, in fact, Hume's view is only superficially similar to Gurdjieff's. First, Hume's thesis is a non-empirical or a priori claim based on the nature of knowledge, whereas Gurdjieff's is an empirical description of the human situation. Second, this first difference reveals itself in the fact that, whereas Hume's theory characterizes a necessary truth about the very idea of the self, in Gurdjieff's system a person can acquire a permanent self through a long struggle of self-observation and self-remembering. Hume's claim is a priori and Gurdjieff's is empirical. In Gurdjieff, the claim that we are a plurality of personalities is a function of the fact that we are controlled by external circumstances, and this brings us to the next point.

c) Being Mechanical

According to Gurdjieff, a person is like a machine (SM, p.154). All of our actions, thoughts and feelings depend upon external influences, rather than on our own will. In this sense, our actions are automatic or mechanical.

Gurdjieff also uses the term 'automatic' to refer to any action that is performed without self-consciousness. This is a crucial idea because the aim of the work is freedom and, to be free, one must be conscious (FW, p.37). Bringing these two ideas together, we live mechanically because our actions are merely automatic reactions to external circumstances based on our likes and dislikes, and our actions are externally determined in this way because we have such a low level of consciousness. Because we are asleep and unaware of the factors controlling us, we have no choice but to react mechanically according to the effects of external influences on our desires.

d) Lack of a Will

So far we have discussed three characteristics of human psychology: we are asleep; we lack a unified self; we live mechanically or automatically. There are different aspects of the same point, namely that we lack a self-conscious will. The self-conscious will is the real self that we normally lack and which is required in order to have mastery of our feelings and inner states. The evidence for this lack of will is precisely that we are unable to control our feelings, unable to remember ourselves, that our so-called actions are mechanical reactions based on our likes and dislikes, and that we identify ourselves with our feelings and roles. For example, many people are terrified at the sight of a 'small timid mouse,' and yet usually experience no terror before the inevitability of death (Bel. p.1224). If we had a will, then we would be able to overcome these deficiencies and contradictions through our own volition.

Contrast with Kant

In claiming that we are not free and only have the illusion of choice, Gurdjieff is apparently denying an important strand in Western thought that finds prominence in the philosophies of Kant (1724–1804) and Sartre (1905-1980), both of whom stress the importance of our being free. Kant, in particular, argues that freedom of the will is a precondition of human action; the capacity to choose is what makes certain movements of the human body actions, as opposed to mere movements and as such, this capacity is a necessary condition of responsibility and morality. The suggestion that the ideas of Gurdjieff and Kant are in contradiction is apparently reinforced by the fact that Gurdjieff claims 'Man cannot do.' Because we are not free, strictly speaking, our behavior does not consist of actions.

However, this particular way of contrasting Gurdjieff and Kant is misleading in two ways. First, whereas for Kant freedom is absolute, for Gurdjieff it is a question of degree. For instance, we are freer in waking daytime hours than we are when we are asleep. Ouspensky writes:

> Certainly, if we begin to think philosophically that there is no such thing as freedom, then there is nothing left but to die (FW, p.37).

Evidently, Gurdjieff's point is that we can become freer than we are now from reactions to circumstances based on our likes and dislikes.

The illusion is to mistake blind mechanical reactions based on our likes and dislikes with free choice. 'Things either attract or repel' us and we call it 'will' (FW, p.39). Even when we make an effort to break a habit or to act contrary to our likes, this is still an attraction or repulsion to something. Second, the Gurdjieffian claim that humans are machines is in the final analysis an analogy. We are not machines, in the sense that we have the potential to become freer.

However, in order that these last two points do not conceal the radical nature of Gurdjieff's claim, let me repeat something said earlier: namely that, in a sense, human beings do not exist at all. What exists is a complex mechanism. This has many implications. For instance, all talk of morality is misleading, because morality requires that we can freely control our state (see Chapter 7). As a consequence, the first focus of the work in order to become freer is to study the complex working of this machine (SM, p.349).

e) Self Deception

The four characteristics of our everyday life are different aspects of the same phenomena. The last feature, which is that we lie to ourselves about our state, is one of the main obstacles to change. In effect, it is what maintains us in our present condition.

If Gurdjieff's views are correct then, we are not really persons at all, bur rather sleeping machines. If he is right, then I do not really exist, but rather there is a fragmented collection of automatic reactions, which I mistake for a real person. In other words, according to Gurdjieff, we are thoroughly and shockingly deluded about our current condition. This mistaken conception of ourselves perpetuates that unreal state.

Gurdjieff calls this delusion a form of lying or self-deceit. However, we should note that an illusion is not necessarily a self-deception, because the latter carries the additional idea that one is lying to oneself. In fact, Gurdjieff claims that we do lie to ourselves. In some sense, we already know that we are asleep and that we live mechanically (SM, p.153). We know, but pretend not to. In particular, we pretend to ourselves that we are awake and freely able to perform actions from our own will. We lie to ourselves so frequently that we hardly know what sincerity is (SM, p.249; Bel, p.378). Sincerity with oneself is harder than it is with a friend.

However, because self-deceit keeps us in our current condition, we need to undermine that self-deceit in order to transform ourselves.

> Sincerity may be the key, which will open the door through which one part can see another part (Gurdjieff, 1975, p.145)

When self-deceit is destroyed, a person begins to see the difference between the mechanical and the conscious in him or herself (SM, p.282). This process is described in the next two chapters.

Conclusion

According to Gurdjieff, 'today, civilization...has wrenched man from the normal conditions in which he should be living' (Gurdjieff, 1971, p.26). Most humans live mechanically in a state of hypnotic sleep. We are sleeping machines. This is a function of our low level of consciousness and of our lack of will. However, we can acquire a will and become conscious, but this requires effort and work. These are two aspects of the same struggle.

2

The Possibility of Transformation

We have described the depressing everyday state in which, according to Gurdjieff, we normally live. Now, we need to describe those aspects of human psychology that permit us to move beyond that state and become more real, free, and conscious. We shall describe the work processes that are required for evolution in the next chapter.

Since, according to Gurdjieff, we are normally no more than machines, self-transformation as such is strictly impossible. However, it is possible for the human machine to become aware of the complex mechanisms that constitute its everyday functioning and, in this way, transformation in a group with the aid of a teacher may be possible. This is a theme that we shall return to later.

Observation of the working of the human machine is based first on the division of the centers. In contrast to the delusions concerning the self described in the previous chapter, the division of a person into various centers is not illusory (FW, p.3 & 60). According to Gurdjieff, we really are so divided because the centers function in quite different ways from each other and, as a consequence, our understanding of ourselves must be based on these centers. Given this, we can also understand the distinction between personality and essence and the difference between different levels of persons and, thereby, the idea of higher levels of consciousness.

The Centers

In *Beelzebub's Tales*, Gurdjieff describes humans as three-brained beings, contrasting humans with two-brained beings, vertebrates, and one-brained beings, invertebrates (Bel, p.143-6). According to Gurdjieff, some ways of dividing human functions are correct, while others are false (Gurdjieff, 1975, p.230). Gurdjieff distinguishes three functions or centers: the intellectual, emotional, and the bodily. Each one of which is like a separate mind that can function independently of the others (Gurdjieff, 1971, p.27-8; SM, p.115).

In practice, distinguishing the three functions can be very difficult. We normally assume that people are much more alike than they really are. People differ in the way that they experience the three functions. For example, some people perceive through their intellectual minds; others through their feelings and others through sensation or the bodily function. Some people call their thoughts, or intellectual perceptions, 'feelings.' While other people will call their feelings 'thoughts,' and yet others their sensations, 'feelings' (SM, p.107).

Furthermore, the same action can originate in different centers. A good example is the drill soldier. The young recruit has to perform the drill with his thinking and the old campaigner performs it through the moving or bodily center, and for this reason is better at it. In our present state, each center functions automatically or mechanically (SM p.114). However, when an action is observed, it becomes less automatic.

These three centers can work harmoniously, each performing its proper function (Gurdjieff, 1971, p.28). For example, the centers work together in artistic creation (FW, p.60). However, they are usually mixed up and interfere with each other's work. For example, people can become emotional at times when it would be better to act without feeling (FW, p.67). When the emotional center tries to do the work of the thinking one, a person becomes nervous and feverish. In contrast, when the thinking center tries to feel, then the person acts slowly and deliberately, even when speed is required (SM 109). Once the centers work harmoniously, each according to its nature, then a person can begin to create in him or herself higher states of consciousness.

In some contexts, Gurdjieff also distinguishes between the instinctive and the moving functions, bringing the list to a total of four (SM, p.114). The beating of the heart, digestion and the circulation of the blood are properly called instinctive because they are innate. Reflexes also count as instinctive, because they do not have to be learned. In contrast, the actions of the moving center are acquired. The moving center is imitative; young animals and babies learn by naturally imitating their parents, without reasoning.

Sex Center

In addition to these four centers, Gurdjieff sometimes adds a fifth, the sex center (SM, p.257). Much of what he says about the other centers applies to this one too. The abuse of sex consists primarily in the other centers using sexual energy and the sexual center using the energies from the other centers. For example, the use of sexual energy by the thinking and emotional centers is recognized by a particular 'taste,' or fervor, or vehemence, which is generally useless (SM, p.258). As a consequence of this mixing, our activities are often motivated by sexual energy. For instance, we are often motivated by sexual energy to attend social gatherings, for example when we go to church or to the theatre (SM, p.254).

In the chapter 'The Holy Planet Purgatory' in *Beelzebub*, Gurdjieff claims that sexual energy can be a source of fuel for the higher centers or bodies (Bel, p.806-8). He did not, however, lay down any specific rules for the use of such energy (Bennett, 1973, p.233). For some people, sexual abstinence is necessary for the process of development and for others, not. In any case, what is important for the development of a person is abstaining from the misuse of sexual energy by the other centers (SM, p. 256).

Gurdjieff's claim that there are five centers is compatible with the original tripartite division, because the sexual, instinctive and moving centers are parts of what he earlier called the bodily center.

Personality and Essence

In order to develop towards higher states of consciousness, a person needs to overcome the incredible power that his or her personality has over his or her essence (SM, p.161). The essence of a person is what is his or her own, the inherited character and nature of the individual. Personality is what is not his or her own. It has come from upbringing, exterior impressions and imitation. 'It is like the clothes you wear, your artificial mask...' (Gurdjieff, 1975, p. 143). This distinction is itself based on the centers. The center of gravity of the personality is the thinking center and that of the essence is the emotional center (Gurdjieff, 1975, p. 137).

Small children have little or no personality. Their likes and wants express their essence. Personality is created through the influence of

15

other people, education, and by the child's imitation of those around him or her (SM, p.161). As personality grows, essence is concealed.

As people grow older and more cultured, their personalities develop, but their essence usually remains child-like. This is because the essence stops receiving the impressions that it needs in order to grow. Often, less cultured persons have a more developed essence. However, this does not mean that a less cultured person has a more favorable condition for self-transformation because work on oneself requires the development of both essence and personality (SM, p.164).

It is possible to separate personality and essence through various techniques, such as hypnosis. In special circumstances, the personality cannot react and the essence must reveal itself. Some narcotics have the effect of putting the personality to sleep without affecting the essence (SM, p.162). In such cases, a person loses his or her ideals and convictions and becomes empty or child-like. As a rule, a person's essence is either primitive, childish and stupid (SM, p.163). Often, people's essences stopped developing at the age of twelve (SM, p.249). For other people, the situation is even worse; their essences have become 'a small and deformed thing,' and some people have essences that are already dead (SM, p.164). Because most of us have an underdeveloped essence, we are timid and full of apprehensions, knowing that we are not what we pretend to be (Bennett, 1973, p.133).

One of the important implications of the distinction between personality and essence for Gurdjieff's teaching is that each person requires an individual program for his or her development. People have different essential natures, and the teacher must be able to set individuals tasks and work, which accord with their essences. Gurdjieff claims that there are several (six or seven) fundamental types of persons, corresponding to different essences. Most of the people we meet are combinations of these different types (SM, p.246-7). Although he does not give examples of such types, he claims that the differences between the types are an important factor in the relationships between the sexes. Because we usually live in our personalities, people are attracted to others at the level of their personalities, even if their essential types are psychologically incompatible (SM, p.254).

The need for individualized work of Gurdjieff's teaching is also emphasized by the idea of a chief fault. Each person's personalities have a central feature, which is like an axis around which these personalities revolve (SM, p.226). For example, Gurdjieff identified one person's chief center as being a tendency to argue with others (SM, p.268). One common chief fault is that we perceive other people's limitations and not our own. Another typical one is self-pity (SM, p.179). The people around a person can often see his or her chief feature even though it remains hidden to the individual him or herself. Nicknames sometimes define chief features very well (SM, p. 267). When a person learns and accepts what his or her chief fault is, then he or she can begin to destroy involuntary manifestations or expressions of that chief feature (SM, p. 267).

To return to the main theme, in order for a person to develop towards higher states of consciousness, the individual's essence has to become alive. Typically, a person's personality is active, and his or her essence is passive. In order that this situation can change, the person has to remove the buffers that separate essence and personality (SM, p.163). However, this process itself requires will, and the personality has no real will. Our personalities are very open to suggestion and are easily influenced. A person's will is part of his or her essence rather than the personality (Bennett, 1973, p.132). In this way, our development must be of the essence.

The Higher Centers

In addition to the five centers mentioned earlier, Gurdjieff sometimes adds two higher centers: the higher emotional and the higher intellectual centers (Bennett, 1973, p.247). In order to tap these higher centers, it is first necessary that the ordinary feeling and thinking centers function properly, so that they can function with higher forms of energy and at much greater speeds. Ouspensky claims that the functioning of these two higher centers is associated with new emotions and thoughts at an intensity and velocity that we could not normally handle (SM, p.194-7). The functioning of these higher centers requires the development of higher bodies, which is explained in Chapter 4. In the language of *Beelzebub's Tales*, Objective Reason cannot function in the normal physical body (Bennett, 1973, p.253).

Levels of Persons

Paralleling the distinction between the different centers, Gurdjieff distinguishes different levels of human existence. A human being number 1 is dominated by material and bodily considerations. This does not preclude the person having intellectual interests but, typically, he or she will make judgments that are based on quantity rather than quality. Human beings of the second type are dominated by the feelings and tend to be emotionally exaggerated, with irrational enthusiasms and with flamboyant likes and dislikes. However, not all people of the second kind are so obviously emotional. Their chief characteristic is the tendency to trust feelings rather than material factors and ideas. Persons of the third type are predominantly intellectual. They tend towards abstraction and solving problems with words rather than actions. Intellectual considerations take priority over their bodies and feelings (Bennett, 1973, p.243).

Most of the people we meet belong to one of these three categories. The fourth type of person has the three centers of functions in balance, working harmoniously. This is because he or she has what Gurdjieff calls a permanent center of gravity, which is formed by a commitment to the values required for personal growth, namely to fulfilling his or her obligations. Persons of this fourth group have made the first step towards liberation from egoism. This fourth state is the natural one for humans, although few people have attained that level.

Nevertheless, a person of type four has not reached the full potential of the human being. Persons of type 5 are those who have developed a second, finer body, which Gurdjieff calls the kesdjan body, which can acquire Objective Reason (Chapter III, *Beelzebub's Tales*). Only persons who have developed a kesdjan body can be said to survive the death of the physical body and can be said to have a real self or will.

Bennett compares persons of type 6 with the Bodhisatva of Mahayana Buddhism and with the great saints of Christianity and Islam, who were concerned with the welfare of humanity as a whole (Bennett, 1973, p.245). Persons of type 7 are fully liberated from the human condition, including their own individuality and, in this sense, can be said to have died (Bennett, 1973, p.245). Persons of type 7 have a developed higher intellectual center, which Gurdjieff calls higher Objective Reason in *Beelzebub's Tales* and which is only two levels below the Absolute Reason of the Creator (Bennett, 1973, p.253). To understand these comparisons, we need to examine Gurdjieff's views concerning the levels of consciousness.

Consciousness

As we described earlier, Gurdjieff distinguishes four states or levels of consciousness, of which we normally live in the first two, even though we may have flashes of the third and even of the fourth.

The first two states of consciousness are respectively normal sleep, and ordinary waking consciousness, The third state is self-consciousness, or consciousness of one's being, which naturally humans should have, but which we lack because of 'the wrong conditions' of our lives (SM, p.141). It can be made permanent only through training and self-remembering, through which a person becomes aware of both him or herself and his/her machine (Gurdjieff, 1975, p.79).

18

Gurdjieff calls the fourth level of awareness objective consciousness. In this state, a person 'can see things as they are' (SM, p.142). In this objective state of consciousness, one is directly aware, all at once, of everything one knows about a particular thing (SM, p.155 and FW, p.151).

Gurdjieff says that, in the second state of consciousness, humans live in a subjective world of 'I like,' 'I do not like,' I want,' and 'I do not want.' They do not see the real world (SM, p.143). This suggests that the third state of consciousness is objective in the sense that one can perceive oneself without the interference of desires and imagination, and that, in the fourth state of consciousness, one can perceive the world without such interference (FW, p.106). We also find within the writings on Gurdjieff, the suggestion echoed by Heraclitus (540-480 BC) when he wrote:

> For the waking there is one common world, but, when asleep each person, turns away to a private one (22B89).

Perhaps, even at the risk of circularity, the best way to understand these higher states of consciousness is as follows. In the higher states, one is no longer glued to one's moods, likes and dislikes and, therefore, these likes and dislikes no longer cloud our awareness and form a barrier to prevent us from perceiving reality.

Conclusion

Although Gurdjieff paints a pessimistic picture of the current state of most people, he insists that human potential is very great (SM, p.145). In other words, a human is a natural being sunk to the level of machine with supernatural potential (Bennett, 1973, p.245).

This stark contrast suggests a set of fundamental questions about Gurdjieff's teaching. How can a person who lives in a set of artificial personalities develop his or her essence? How can a being is deeply asleep wake him or herself up? In short, how can a machine make itself a person? These questions will be addressed in the next chapter.

3
The Work

The study of human psychology should be directed towards the self-transformation of human beings, or to our evolution. The word 'evolution' here does not refer, of course, to the process of natural selection, but to the process of acquiring a real self. We are incomplete and, to complete ourselves, we have to develop consciousness and will. To express this idea, Bennett quotes Goethe: 'One must strive to become what one is' (Bennett, 1973, p.239). How can we transform ourselves? In brief, we must begin with what we can control directly, our thoughts, rather than our emotions, which currently lie beyond our direct control.

1) Self Observation

The first step is to become more aware that one is a sleeping machine. One of the chief obstacles to self-evolution is self-deception or being willfully mistaken about oneself. Overcoming this tendency requires self-observation, which brings a person to realize the necessity for self-change (SM, p.145).

Self-observation is the first stage on the path of acquiring a self. In the beginning, it should not consist of too much analysis, in order to avoid the danger of becoming distracted by or engrossed in one's own thoughts (SM, p.105). Rather, it should consist of recording one's states and differentiating the different functions mentioned in Chapter 2. For instance, one can try to differentiate thought and feeling referring one's impressions to the appropriate categories when obvious. This

20

will help one identify cases in which the functions work incorrectly, for instance when the thinking center pretends that it is feeling something.

It is worth spending some on this point. If the feeling center habitually tries to think, then this can be a cause of nervousness and, when it is the other way around, a person reacts too slowly and deliberately. The intellectual mind cannot understand feelings. When the moving center works for the thinking one, a person reads and listens inattentively (SM, p.110). Daydreaming, worrying and imagining are also results of a malfunctioning of the centers. The thinking center repeats pleasant or unpleasant experiences for the sake of the emotional center. They are thoughts motivated by the feeling center. The one center hypnotizes the other (N1, p.87).

Knowing oneself also requires studying one's habits, a difficult process that requires trying to free oneself from one's routines (SM, p.111). It requires a struggle that by itself will not result in change, but which permits self-observation. For instance, observing how one normally walks requires changing one's habitual way of walking. Similar points apply to the study of the routine ways in which one expresses negative emotions, such as complaint. The overall aim of such self-observation is to come the realization that one lives like an automaton in hypnotic sleep.

In the beginning of this process, self-observation must be based on an understanding of the fundamental principles of the activities of the human machine (SM, p.106). Typically, people want to change only one part of themselves. However, everything in the human machine is interconnected, and every function is counterbalanced by some other (SM, p.108). This means that isolated change is not fruitful. For example, suppose that an individual is forgetful and absent-minded. For years, he struggles against this fault and manages to overcome it. However, this alteration may bring another change, which he himself may not notice; for example, he may have become more pedantic, fault finding and irritable. This does not mean that loss of absent-mindedness will always be compensated by irritability. In another person, the counterbalance might be envy or something else (SM. p.108).

When a person comes to recognize the need for more than just self-observation, but also the need for work on him or herself, then the nature of self-observation must change. Prior to this realization, the person has only studied the workings of different parts of his or her machine (such as the centers) rather like an impartial witness. Now with this realization, he or she must observe the whole machine. He or she must take mental photographs of his or her whole state at characteristic and interesting moments (SM, p.146). In this way, the person will begin to perceive him or herself as he or she really is.

21

This process requires that the person divide him or herself into two persons: the real me and the other. This will result in the feeling that he or she is two persons: the real self and the collection of artificial personalities that usually control it (SM, p.147-8). In other words, it requires that the person not say 'I' to his or her passing moods and feelings (N1, p.61). If one says 'I am feeling negative,' then one identifies oneself with the feeling, and there is no separation between the 'I' and the feeling. If instead one affirms 'It is feeling negative' then there is a division between the observed and the observing (N1, p.305).

This stage in one's development is fraught with the danger that one will divide oneself according to one's personal likes and dislikes, assigning the characteristics of oneself that one dislikes to the artificial personalities. Furthermore, the individual may feel at the total mercy of this other, i.e. the collection of personalities that control the real self, and horrified at his or her powerlessness. At this stage of the process, a person does not have the capacity to properly distinguish the artificial and the real in him or herself and, therefore, needs guidance (SM, p.149). This dividing of the self requires that the person no longer identify him or herself with this other, and the struggle against identification makes remembering oneself both possible and necessary. In other words, at this stage, observing oneself ultimately requires remembering oneself.

2) Negative Emotions

Before examining the central idea of remembering oneself, we must look at the role of negative emotions. According to Gurdjieff, negative emotions, such as anger, jealousy, self-pity, and irritation, are not a necessary part of our make-up because they are not an essential function of any center. This means that they can be eliminated. Negative emotions essentially involve identification and negative imagination, both of which can be eradicated (FW, p.70). This does not mean that they can expelled by thought alone, but rather that the first step to their elimination is the realization that they are dispensable. In other words, we can stop justifying them to ourselves, for example, pretending that they are forced upon us by circumstances or by the behavior of others. For instance, we often think that we cannot bear the unpleasant manifestations of other people (SM, p.367; Bel, p.242). Or, for example, we falsely justify negative emotions to ourselves by thinking that, without venting them, we shall bottle them up, or that we need to let off steam (FW, p.71). Second, we can realize that negative emotions are worse than useless. Expressing negative emotions wastes our energy, which could be used in self-remembering or in becoming conscious (FW, p.69). In these ways, right thinking can help us overcome negative emotions.

We can destroy negative emotions first by having the right attitude towards or right thinking about them as mentioned above. Second, we can try to stop expressing them. Not expressing negative emotions does not consist in suppressing them, but rather in finding reasons for not expressing them (FW, p.73). In general, negative emotions arise because we blame other people for what happens to us and, to counter-act this, we can try to understand that we are responsible for what happens to us and for what we feel (Gurdjieff, 1975, p.162; FW, p.76). For example, we become irritated by the mechanical reactions of other people only because we ourselves are mechanical.

Thirdly, we can study ourselves as we struggle not to express such emotions and resist our habitual reactions that involve such expression. Such struggle constitutes a resistance that makes self-observation possible.

Fourth, we can fight the emotions themselves, rather than just their expression, by trying to not identify ourselves with them (FW, p.75). The emotional center believes that only the feeling of the present moment is real, and this leads us to identify ourselves with our current emotional state (FW, p. 369). Identification is a state in which one loses oneself in something that attracts or repels us (FW, p. 126). It is identification that causes us to be asleep.

The first element of the fight against self-identification is to be aware that we identify ourselves. This requires an inner separation of the negative emotion and the 'I' (N1, p.61). We need to catch ourselves in more obvious moments of identification to begin to realize how much it pervades our lives (FW, p. 124). We can be aware of identification when it is weaker or stronger than usual (FW, p. 127).

The second element of the struggle against identification is self-remembering. However, the identification involved in having negative emotions makes self-remembering impossible at such moments. Nevertheless, one can slowly train oneself so that negative emotions remind one of the need to be in a state of self-remembering (FW, p. 359).

3) Self-Remembering

Self-remembering is the cornerstone of the process of psychological transformation. The other processes of self-study and the struggle against negative emotions are preparations for self-remembering. In Gurdjieff's system, self-remembering is the necessary antidote to the mechanical state of sleep, which results from identification and in which we spend our lives. Since this mechanical sleep prevents us from being able to really act, self-remembering is an important aspect of Gurdjieff's view of morality (see Chapter 7). 'Self-remembering is a method of awakening' (FW, p.111).

When one observes something normally, one's attention is directed to that thing, whether that it is something external or some internal state. In contrast, when one observes something while self-remembering, one's attention is divided in two: one attends to the thing and to oneself (SM, p.119).

Self-remembering is not the same as ordinary self-consciousness, because the latter is a permanent state (FW, p.122). In contrast, self-remembering is an act of will by which one creates a higher state of consciousness in oneself (FW, p.112). It consists of being able to stop identifying oneself and of being aware of oneself at will.

Real self-remembering requires high level emotional energy (FW, p. 111). However, we have no control over the working of even our lower emotional center. For this reason, at first, we should try to realize that we are asleep and that we cannot remember ourselves. The more continuous this realization is, the closer we will be to actually remembering ourselves. For example, we can notice that everyday consciousness has different degrees (FW, p.109). Then, we can work indirectly to remember ourselves, by trying to control our thoughts and divide our attention by putting in the center of our thoughts the feeling of 'I' and 'I am' (FW, p.114). For example, we can try to stop thinking as a way to help us remember ourselves (FW, p. 117).

Remembering oneself awakens emotions and, by degrees, it will become more emotional and less intellectual (FW, p.113-4). Furthermore, we should try to remember ourselves in moments of strong emotion as an antidote to identification (FW, p. 118).

According to Gurdjieff, our normal inability to remember ourselves for more than perhaps a few moments is evidence of our hypnotized low level of consciousness. Ouspensky links our inability to remember ourselves with our usually poor memory. He claims that one remembers directly and vividly those moments when one remembers oneself, and that other memories tend to be impersonal, i.e. only that such and such happened to me. In other words, they embody a third person perspective rather than a first person one.

4) Effort

Gurdjieff emphasizes the need for sacrifice in the work. Of course, we can sacrifice only what we have. Thus, the work requires us to sacrifice our illusions, daydreams, and our needless suffering (SM, p.274). We need to make efforts to overcome the mental inertia that helps to keep us asleep and mechanical (FW, p.119). One of the most difficult efforts required of a person is to stop lying. We lie so much that we are often not aware of it. Another effort is the conquest of fears that are usually linked to the person's lies (SM, p.230).

The personal work of each individual consists in struggling again his or her chief fault (SM, p.226). For this reason, work must be personalized, and there can be no general system for the work. For example, if a person talks too much, then he or she must learn to be silent. Another person might have the tendency to keep silent when he or she needs to talk. What is useful for one person might be harmful for another (SM, p.226). Furthermore, a person cannot identity his or her own chief fault. The teacher has to do this and show him or her how to overcome that fault. Typically, the teacher will set the pupil specific tests or tasks that touch the individual's chief fault and, as a result, some people leave the work indignant (SM, p.228).

Every effort that a person makes increases the demands that the teacher makes on him or her. It is a mistake to think that past efforts merit fewer efforts in the future. On the contrary, the fewer efforts a person has made in the past, the less the teacher will demand of him or her in the future (SM, p.230).

Gurdjieff not only stresses the need for sacrifice and effort; he also points out the need for super-efforts through which a person can tap huge reservoirs of energy. Super-efforts consist in continuing with an effort precisely at the point at which one feels one can go on no more. In this way, rather than allowing superficial pools of energy to replenish, the organism has to draw upon a deeper reserve, which Gurdjieff calls the large accumulator (SM, p.235).

An example of a super-effort would be, if after having walked 25 miles home, instead of having supper in the warmth of my home, I decide to walk an extra two miles before returning home again (SM, p. 347). It is even harder to make such super-efforts when a teacher demands them.

5) Exercises

The work has a very important physical or bodily aspect. Our psychological states are usually determined by our bodily states, including those bodily functions that we are not usually aware of. In the Prieuré, most of Gurdjieff's students were assigned heavy physical labor as part of their work. They had to clear and plant the woods, build roads, construct and repair buildings, as well as performing the household chores, such as taking care of the animals, cleaning, washing, and cooking. During this period of frenzied activity, Gurdjieff gave his groups exercises in fasting, explaining that the work consists in intentional suffering (SM, p.356 and 358). These hardships permitted self-observation in new conditions.

Gurdjieff also taught his students various postures and exercises. He claimed that a person is unable to change the form of his or her thinking and feeling without altering his/her repertoire of postures and movements. Our feelings and moods are intimately connected with our postures and movements (Gurdjieff, 1975, p.161; SM, p.352). The bodily, emotional and thinking centers work together, but usually in an automatic way; the movements provide a break in such habits and thereby provide an opportunity for self-observation. Gradually, the power of the body over the emotions and thought is weakened (Bennett, 1973, p.228).

Gurdjieff also taught 'the movements' partly because we waste enormous amounts of energy through unnecessary muscular tensions. Therefore, a person must learn to feel such tensions and relax them, starting with the muscles of the face (SM, p.350). We unnecessarily waste muscular energy. For example, even when we are sitting doing nothing, the muscles of our legs, back, neck and stomach are tensed. Even in sleep, our muscles are tense (SM, p.196). Relaxing these muscles requires becoming aware of bodily functions that are usually automatic.

The rhythmic exercises, gymnastics and dances that Gurdjieff taught were usually accompanied by music, either that he had learned in his travels or of his own composition (SM, p.358 & p.372). These dances were known as the movements and were performed publicly in Tbilisi, France and the United States (Bennett, 1973, p.222). Gurdjieff first initiated his students to these movements in Tuapse in 1918; they become an important part of the work at the Prieuré until his accident in 1924. They were resumed in 1928 until his death in 1949.

Gurdjieff also used the stop exercise as part of his practical training. At the word 'stop,' all pupils had to instantly freeze their position, including their facial muscles, eyes, thoughts and feelings (SM, p. 351-6). The purpose of this exercise was to make the pupils aware of their state while in the transition from one posture to another (Gurdjieff, 1975, p.156; Bennett, 1973, p.227). It was an exercise in self-observation and control.

The primary aim of these exercises and the movements was to help the development of the dancers rather than to perform a spectacle for an audience. A developed person must have the thinking, feeling and bodily functions working in harmony. The movements help achieve the required balance. Furthermore, the dances or movements were used to train the attention. For instance, to perform the complex movements it is necessary to attend directly to different parts of the body, without the intervention of thought (Bennett, 1973, p.229). The dances were also an exercise in self-control, to help the person develop his or her will. Some of the dances also had a symbolic meaning.

In addition to these general lines of work for the whole group, Gurdjieff gave his students individualized tasks, corresponding to his or her essence type and designed to overcome the chief fault of each (SM, p.241). These tasks would be assigned to an individual for a time and then be changed.

6) Groups

The individual cannot escape from the prison of egoism on his or her own. One needs help from someone who has already escaped (SM, p.30). In other words, a person cannot awake by him or herself. Theoretically, a group of people could make an agreement that the first of them to awake should rouse the others, but, even then, it is still possible that they will all fall asleep at the same time and dream that they are waking up (SM, p.144). We have accumulated thousands of sleep compelling habits that need to be overcome (SM, p.144). So, in reality, such a group requires a teacher who is not asleep.

The work begins with self-study. In a group, the members can exchange their observations and learn from each other (SM, p.223). In this way, each individual has the possibility to progress more rapidly. Furthermore, in a group, there is a rule of common responsibility (SM, p. 231). Each must be responsible for the development of the others. This means that there can be no personal interests that are likely to hinder the work of the group as a whole. Furthermore, there can be no personal animosities, which would be an obstacle to the mutual responsibility (SM, p.231).

Being in a group requires that the members abide by certain conditions or rules. One is to not speak to others outside of the group about the details of the work, and this requires struggling against one's tendency to chat (SM, p.224). Another rule is that one must tell the teacher of the group the whole truth in order to learn sincerity. Another is that each member of the group must remember the aim with which he or she came to the group.

To help other people, one must first learn to help oneself. Many people want to help others as a way to avoid working on themselves (SM, p.103). It is pleasant to think that one can help others, but this can be a way of being insincere with oneself. The phrases 'love of mankind' and 'altruism' have meaning only when a person has the capacity to choose whether to be an egoist or an altruist or whether to love others or not (see Chapter 7).

The Fourth Way

Gurdjieff contrasts his work methods, which he calls the fourth way, with the first three ways, that of the fakir, the monk and the yogi. In each case, the aim is to develop a true self. The first way is that of the fakir, which consists of willful struggle with the body through torturous exercises. The inherent limitation of this method is that, even if the person achieves the development of the will, the emotional and intellectual functions will remain underdeveloped. Similarly, the way of the monk, which focuses on the development of religious emotions, such as the feeling of serving and loving God, in order to attain an inner unity, is inherently limited to only one of the three centers. The way of the yogi concentrates on the development of the intellect or mind, but once again, it ignores the development of the other two centers. Furthermore, these first three ways require a person to renounce normal life.

In contrast, the fourth way does not require such renunciation. It uses the conditions of everyday life because these conditions reflect the condition or state of the individual, thereby providing the opportunity for self-observation. In the Chapter 'India,' Gurdjieff repudiates the idea that one can learn to bear the unpleasant manifestations of other people by removing oneself from the world, both physically and psychologically (Bel, p.242-3).

Furthermore, the fourth way permits the person to work on developing all three centers at once. In that sense, it is more holistic than the first three ways. It also permits individualized work, so that each person works in a way that is most useful to his or her condition. Moreover, the fourth way is based on the need for understanding rather than blind faith. A person must satisfy him or herself as to the truth of what is taught because this is a requirement of understanding the processes involved and the required results (SM, p.45-50 and p.312).

4

The Cosmos

The universe consists of different manifestations and concentrations of energy, which flow from the Absolute and which are all interconnected. As they flow out from the Absolute, these emanations of energy become more or less dense in discrete steps, which constitute different levels of being. At each level of being, there are different units of wholeness, each of which constitutes a different cosmos, and each of which is alive. Energy is transmitted between the levels, in accordance with two fundamental laws, the law of three and the law of seven (Bel, p.137). Thus, Gurdjieff presents a picture of the universe that is neither strictly monist nor dualist, that is holistic without being pantheistic and that is organic, without ignoring the idea of mechanism.

The primary purpose of Gurdjieff's teaching, whether it concerns human psychology or metaphysical cosmology, is to help humans evolve and become complete (FW, 112). However, it is impossible to study the human condition without investigating the nature of the universe (SM, p.75). This is because each individual mirrors the whole world, in the sense that the laws that govern the universe also apply to us. The individual human is like a miniature universe (Bel, p.775). The cosmology of Gurdjieff's system is based on five fundamental ideas, which I shall describe, without evaluating them.

29

1) Levels of Energy

The first basic idea of Gurdjieff's cosmology is that there are different levels of energy. This is linked to the second idea that these are also different levels of being.

Regarding energy, Gurdjieff's cosmology is, in a sense, materialist. Everything is composed of matter, which is not separate from energy (Bel, p.138; FW, p.213). There are no non-material beings. However, not all matter is of a piece. The universe as a whole consists of different levels of existence that are composed of matter of different densities or energies of different vibrations. Higher worlds are composed of matter that is finer, and lower worlds of matter of a greater density, or that is coarser (FW, p.213). Finer levels of matter are more energetic than the coarser ones (FW, p. 220). Matter is in a permanent state of vibration, and the rate of vibration is in inverse ratio to the density of matter. For example, at the level of the Absolute, the vibrations are the most rapid, and at the level of mineral matter, they are the most slow (SM, p.87).

Each level of matter has its own atom, which 'are indivisible only on a given plane' (SM, p.87). For example, the atoms of World 6 consist of six atoms of the Absolute and their movements are correspondingly slower. Thus, even the Absolute itself is material. It has a weight that, in principle, could be measured (SM, p.86).

Gurdjieff claims that there are seven discrete levels of energy or matter, of which we are only directly acquainted with two. These levels of energy are:

1.	World 1	The Absolute
2.	World 3	All Worlds
3.	World 6	All suns (galactic)
4.	World 12	The Sun (solar)
5.	World 24	All planets (planetary)
6.	World 48	The Earth (organic life)
7.	World 96	Lunar (mineral or material)

(This table is based on Ouspensky (SM, p.82 and p.87; my parenthetic additions are to help the reader connect this table with another one given below). The idea of levels of matter is related to that of natural laws, which specify the inescapable conditions of existence at each level. Higher worlds are subject to fewer natural laws than the lower ones in the following progression: 1, 3, 6, 12, 24, 48, 96. For example, the Absolute is subject to only one law, namely its own will (SM, p.83). The three laws that govern World 3 are directly subject to the direct will of the Absolute. However, of the 48 laws applicable at the level of the earth, only those three come directly from the Absolute. Note that Gurdjieff himself does not provide clear examples of the 48 laws which govern our world. He claims that these laws cannot be defined in ordinary language in a way that permits us to catalogue them (SM, p.246). Nevertheless, Bennett tries to describe these laws based on the idea of the triad or the law of three, which is described below, as applied to the will (see Bennett, 1961).

The claim that a different number of laws govern the levels of energy is important primarily because it provides background for the statement that human evolution is a movement towards greater freedom. Higher worlds are freer than the lower ones and are less mechanical because they are subject to fewer laws, and human development consists in attaining consciousness of and an existence in these higher worlds.

The physical sciences can study matter only of types 48 and 96, and those with a level higher can be known only through their psychological effects on persons. The matter of World 24 is too rarefied to be considered material at all from the point of view of physics. In other words, matter on a higher plane does not seem material from the point of view of the lower levels. Gurdjieff says that it is impossible for persons at levels 1, 2, and 3 to directly know the finer levels of matter (FW, p.213).

Matter that possesses the characteristics of materiality known to us is itself divided into several states according to its density: solid, liquid, gas and radiant energy, such as light and magnetism (SM, p.88). In other words, there exist levels within each level. This accords with the idea of vibrations within vibrations discussed below.

The finer forms of matter permeate the coarser ones analogous to the way that water may saturate a piece of wood. The finer matter of higher worlds penetrates the matter of this world (SM, p. 88). This point is of vital importance to Gurdjieff's system because human development consists in acquiring bodies of higher levels of energy. In other words, as a person becomes more able to consciously remember him or herself, he or she transforms the energies that comprise the working of the body in such a way that more and more of the finer energies are produced, as will be described briefly below. These finer energies pervade the coarser body and, finally, coalesce or crystallize into a new, finer body within the material body. Through this process, the person can acquire something akin to a soul that can survive physical death and, the process of development can continue after the death of our coarse physical bodies. Gurdjieff calls the first finer body, the kesdjan.

2) Levels of Being

The second basic idea of Gurdjieff's cosmology is that these different levels of energy actually constitute different levels of being or wholeness. Ouspensky sometimes explains this idea as follows. Humans belong to the earth, which itself belongs to the planetary world. Planets belong to a solar system and are part of the solar world. The sun is part of the Milky Way galaxy, which is part of the galactic world. The galaxy itself belongs to the world of all galaxies. Finally, there is the Absolute in which everything is one (FW, p.195 and SM, p.76).

However, this explanation mixes two different concepts. One is the familiar idea that galaxies are composed of solar systems, and solar systems are composed of suns and planets. The universe is composed of parts and wholes of different sizes. The other is the additional and unfamiliar idea that some of these parts of the whole constitute worlds within worlds, or distinct cosmoses, each corresponding to a different level of materiality or energy. In other words, there are different levels of unity or wholeness. The world as a totality is divided into seven categories of cosmoses, one category or world within the other (SM, p. 86). The different cosmoses are:

		Ouspensky	Gurdjieff
1.	World 1	The Absolute	Endlessness
2.	World 3	All worlds	Protocosmos
3.	World 6	Galaxies	Megalocosmos
4.	World 12	Suns	Defterocosmos
5.	World 24	Planets	Tritocosmos
6.	World 48	Organisms	Tertartocomos
7.	World 96	Atoms or cells	Microcosmos

The terminology in the column marked 'Ouspensky' is adapted from *In Search of the Miraculous*, page 205. The column marked 'Gurdjieff' is derived from *Beelzebub's Tales* (Bel, p.760-1). For more details, see the appendix below.

The above table represents different degrees of unity or wholeness. The general idea is best understood in terms of an analogy. In World 48, we regard the single organism as a whole natural individual, and the smallest living part of that organism is a cell, which is a unit in World 96. Analogously, in World 24, a whole individual would be a planet, and the wholeness of an organism, such as an animal, would be akin to that of a cell as from the point of view of World 48. Analogously, from the point of view of World 12, the only real individuals or natural whole entities would be suns or solar systems. From this point of view, organisms would not count as living individuals at all. In this way, the above table of cosmoses aims to represent the principle of the relativity of wholeness (SM, p.207).

This general idea is linked to the claim, discussed in Chapter 1, that, as we are now, we humans do not really exist at all, or that we do not have a real self. From the point of view of higher worlds, our usual mode of existence in World 48 does not constitute real individuality at all. We can become real at this higher level only by attaining the level of consciousness of higher worlds. This claim is in turn linked to the concept of bodies of different levels of materiality, because each level of consciousness requires the appropriate body.

Gurdjieff claims that everything has a place in the cosmic order and its position in the scale of cosmoses, together with the forces that act on it, determines its characteristics or nature (SM, p.95).

3) Beings

The third basic idea of Gurdjieff's cosmological system is that everything is living (FW, p. 197).

> Each cosmos is a living being which lives, breathes, thinks, feels is born and dies (SM, p.206).

Nothing in the universe is entirely dead or inanimate; instead, there are different levels or degrees of being alive (Gurdjieff, 1975, p.205; SM, p.317). The higher cosmoses represent or contain beings that are more alive and intelligent than we are. According to Gurdjieff, the level of intelligence of a being is a function of the speed of the vibration of the matter out of which it is composed (SM, p.318). In other words, in Gurdjieff's system, higher levels of being and matter represent higher or more divine intelligences. Gurdjieff's term 'degree of vivifyingness' means degrees of being alive (Bel, 139). For this reason, we can regard the beings in World 24, the planets, as angels, and those of World 12, the suns, as archangels (SM, p.324). In his work, *Beelzebub's Tales,* Gurdjieff calls World 3 or the protocosmos, the Sun Absolute (Bel. p.788).

These beings are composed of finer degrees of matter. Thus, strictly speaking, Gurdjieff's assertion is not that the sun we normally perceive is alive, because the sun so perceived is the manifestation at our level of materiality of a higher being, which is actually composed of finer matter. Gurdjieff also claims that, as our consciousness evolves, we can feel the life of the higher and lower levels (FW, p.207).

4) The Two Fundamental Laws

We have mentioned the laws of the universe that characterize the inescapable conditions at the different levels of existence. However, in addition, there are two more fundamental or overarching laws that characterize the functioning of the universe at each level and between the levels. These laws make the universe as a whole what it is (Bel, p.137).

a) The Law of Three

Gurdjieff calls the law of three, 'the triamazikamno' (Bel, p.138-9). According to the law of three, there are three types of forces in any particular reaction: the active, passive and neutralizing or reconciling (SM, p.89; N1, p.108-9). Gurdjieff formulates the law as follows:

> The higher blends with the lower to actualize the middle,
> which becomes higher for the preceding lower and lower for
> the succeeding higher (Bel, p.751).

This version of the law is slightly reminiscent of Hegel's thesis-antithesis-synthesis. However, this characterizes the third neutral force as the outcome or result of a duality, and Gurdjieff's main idea is rather that all interactions require all three types of forces. A duality on its own cannot produce a result. The active and passive forces need to be brought together by the reconciling force in order for an interaction to have an outcome (Gurdjieff, 1975, p.195). Consequently, the third force may be encountered

> either at the point of application of the forces, or in the
> medium, or in the result (SM, p.77).

Gurdjieff claims that contemporary thought only recognizes the existence of two forces, in terms of phenomena, such as force and resistance, positive and negative electricity (SM, p.77). Furthermore, humans are in general third force blind and see the world in dualistic terms (Bennett, 1988, p.47 & Bel, p.1126). This point is especially important in relation to our propensity to think of morality in terms of a dualistic conflict between good and evil (see Chapter 7).

We can best understand the law of three through its psychological applications. For instance, if a person wants to transform him or herself, this desire counts as a positive force. The inertia of his or her habits counts as a passive force. For changes to occur there must be a reconciling force, which could be knowledge of the system. Also, the primary functions or centers work together as a triad: the affirmative force is the intellect; the negative force is the bodily function, and the reconciling force is the emotional center (Bennett, 1973, p.248).

Matter itself can be a vehicle for each of these three forces, or it can be without one of these three forces. In this way, matter can have four states. In the early period, as reported by Ouspensky, Gurdjieff calls matter as a conductor of the active force, 'carbon;' as transmitter of the passive force, 'oxygen;' and as carrier of the third, neutralizing force, 'nitrogen.' Matter that conducts no force is named 'hydrogen.' The point of this classification will be explained shortly.

The law of three works also at the cosmic level. For example, World 1 conducts the active force; World 3, the passive force and World 6, the neutralizing force (Bel, p.779; FW, p.209). The law of three is also important in Gurdjieff's account of the creation, explained in the next chapter,

b) The Law of Seven

Gurdjieff calls the law of seven, the 'heptaparaparshinokh.' The basic idea is that the vibrations that constitute the various processes of the universe are not continuous, but discontinuous. Vibrations do not develop and change uniformly. At certain points, they increase or decrease more slowly. Since higher forms of matter vibrate more quickly, one can refer to this phenomenon at the cosmic level as the discontinuity in ascending and descending vibrations. The law of seven is why the universe consists of discrete levels.

One known instance of this phenomenon, which serves as an analogy for the generic law, is the musical scale. In the modern major scale, there is a semi-tone between each note except between Do and Si and between Fa and Mi. Similarly, in Gurdjieff's system, an octave is divided into seven unequal parts. If the note Do is 1 then Re will be 9/8, Mi 5/4, Fa 4/3, Sol 3/2, la 5/3, Si 15/8, and Do 2. In other words, the increase or change decelerates between Mi and Fa and between Si and Do. Gurdjieff refers to these intervals as Stopinders (Bel, p.750-1). Because of the analogy, the law of seven is called the law of the octave (SM, p.126).

According to Gurdjieff, this law can explain how processes often turn change direction and even turn into their opposites (Gurdjieff, 1975, p.201). For example, our efforts to achieve some goal suddenly weaken, or a peace process can turn sour. A process of evolution can become one of involution (Bel, p.787).

> We never accomplish what we intend doing, in big and little things. We go to Si and return to Do (Gurdjieff, 1975, p.154).

To maintain their intended direction, an activity or a series of vibrations requires an additional shock or energy at the intervals when the relevant vibrations decelerate.

The Cosmic Octave

The law applies in different ways to ascending and descending octaves. In a descending octave, the interval between Si and Do occurs at the beginning, and in a descending one, at the very end. For this reason, descending octaves develop more easily (SM, p.131). In this way, the line of human evolution, which is an ascending octave, is fundamentally different from the ray of creation, which is a descending one (SM, p.134). The first is a process of evolution, by which the 'many' returns to the one, and the second is one of involution, the process of creation by which the one becomes the 'many' (Bennett, 1988, p.51).

In the case of the descending octave that constitutes the Ray of Creation, the first interval between Si and Do, or between Worlds 1 and 3, is covered by the will of the Absolute, which Gurdjieff calls the autoegogratic process. Organic life is the apparatus that fills the interval between Mi and Fa, or the Worlds 24 (all planets) and 48 (the earth). 'Organic life on earth was created to fill the interval between the planets and the earth' (SM, p.138).

The basic octave that constitutes the Ray of Creation has various subsidiary octaves branching off from it. Furthermore, within certain physical limits, each note of an octave can be considered as an octave on another level (Bel, p.830; SM, p.135). In this way, all natural phenomena can be conceived in terms of this law (Bel, p.785).

In his book, *In Search of the Miraculous*, Ouspensky reports Gurdjieff expounding in considerable detail the law of octaves. He combines it with the law of three to yield the so-called table of hydrogens (SM, p.167-177), which aims to show how the different levels of matter may and may not interact (FW, p.232). There is a different exposition of a similar idea in Bennett's book, *The Dramatic Universe*, especially volume 1 (Bennett, 1956). However, these details are beyond the scope of this book. The law of octave can be represented symbolically with the enneagram, a nine sided figure that Gurdjieff used as the logo for his institute (SM, p.286-8).

The main significance of this aspect of Gurdjieff's system is that it means that human development requires additional shocks at the necessary moments if it is not to go astray (Bel, p.789). This is another reason why a person requires a school in order to develop a real self.

5) Food

The fifth idea is what Gurdjieff calls 'the law of reciprocal maintenance,' or 'the trogoautoegocratic-process.' The idea is that there are constant exchanges of energy between the levels of existence, from one level above and to one level below, and vice versa. In this way, the created universe maintains itself and is able to exist in a stable condition despite the destructive effects of time. In other words, entities in the universe feed off each other. This implies that every natural thing serves a purpose in the general cosmos in terms of what it maintains, and humankind is no exception. As a result, the law of reciprocal maintenance indicates the relevance of Gurdjieff's cosmological scheme for the nature of the earth's organic life, and also specifically for human existence.

Organic life transmits energy from the solar system to the earth. This is true in the obvious sense that, for instance, organic life provides the earth with coal and oil (FW, p.197). However, Gurdjieff expands the concept of food to include higher energies, and he claims that the earth needs food in the way that any living being does. Organic life is an apparatus that fills the gap between Mi and Fa, or the Worlds 24 (all planets) and 48 (the earth). It stores and transmits energy to the earth.

In addition to being part of organic life and being an energy transmitter or factory just like any other organic being, humans can play an additional role in the cosmic trogoautoegocratic-process. We can receive, produce and transmit energy to and from the higher worlds. According to Gurdjieff, we can process higher levels of energy in the form of impressions. Impressions are a form of nourishment, like the food that we eat and the air that we breathe. Every impression we receive from our external environment is associated with a vibration and is a form of energy. Because we cannot live even for a moment without these impressions, they constitute a type of food (SM, p.181).

Human beings are factories that can convert coarser energies into finer ones (Bel, p.780; SM, p.179). From our own point of view, this conversion consists in our attaining higher levels of consciousness, which permit and require our bodies to be infused with these finer energies, and which eventually would crystallize into higher bodies. From the cosmic point of view, we are receiving, transforming, and transmitting energies for the development of the sun, and beyond.

The working of the human factory to transform impressions into higher forms of energy can be described in terms of the law of octaves mentioned above (SM, p.181-198). The details need not concern us here, but the upshot is twofold. First, the production of large quantities of higher energies requires the presence of smaller quantities of those same energies (SM, p.189). Second, in accordance with the law of seven, an ascending octave requires external shocks at certain intervals in order to proceed without going astray. In other words, human development requires shocks, which are provided by the energies released when we make the conscious effort to remember ourselves. Self-remembering transforms the quality of the impressions we receive. In this way, higher impressions have a liberating effect on the individual (FW, p.231).

Conclusion

One general principle of Gurdjieff's system is that the created universe is a self-maintaining system, or an 'organic' whole, consisting of different concentrations of matter. In this system, everything is connected, and things at one level serve the energy requirements of things at another through the trogoautoegocratic-process. As a consequence, humankind exists as a part of organic life, which serves the needs of the planet earth. In this way, Gurdjieff replaces the traditional ideas that the rest of the created universe exists for the sake of humankind and that God has created man for His purposes with the claim that humans exist for the sake of other cosmic purposes (Bennett, 1973. p.241). However, at the same time, we humans have the potential to serve higher cosmic energy needs by developing our consciousness and thereby crystallizing higher level bodies, which would allow us to survive the death of our earthly bodies. We are more than soulless machines, but less than immortal souls (Bennett, 1973, p. 245).

Appendix: Various Tables

1) Cosmoses

The table of cosmoses presented earlier is derived from Ouspensky's *In Search of the Miraculous*, p.205:

		Ouspensky	Gurdjieff
1.	World 1	The Absolute	Endlessness
2.	World 3	All worlds	Protocosmos
3.	World 6	Galaxies	Megalocosmos
4.	World 12	Suns	Defterocosmos
5.	World 24	Planets	Tritocosmos
6.	World 48	Organisms	Tertartocomos
7.	World 96	Atoms or cells	Microcosmos

2) Ray of Creation

The table of cosmoses is different from the Ray of Creation, explained by Ouspensky (SM, p. 82 and p.137) on which he bases the division of the different levels of energy or matter (SM, p.87). Also, Ouspensky presents the cosmic application of the law of octaves in terms of the Ray of Creation.

1.	World 1	The Absolute
2.	World 3	All Worlds
3.	World 6	Our galaxy (galactic)
4.	World 12	The Sun (solar)
5.	World 24	The planets of our solar system (planetary)
6.	World 48	The Earth (organic life)
7.	World 96	The Moon (mineral or material)

Ouspensky reports that Gurdjieff explained the differences between the table of cosmoses and the Ray of Creation in the following terms (SM p.206). First, whereas the astronomical Ray of Creation represents the universe from our earth-bound point of view, the table of cosmoses abstracts from that point of view. The first represents our particular ray of creation, implying that creation has many other rays. The descending octave that constitutes our ray of creation terminates in the mineral level of the moon. This means that the moon is less of a being than the earth.

Second, the levels in the Ray of Creation are not permanent; they can change. In other words, the moon and the earth, for example, can evolve. In contrast, the levels represented by the table of cosmoses are fixed. This seems to imply that the levels of matter should be explained in terms of the table of cosmoses rather than the Ray of Creation.

3) The Diagram of Everything Living

Both the table of cosmoses and the Ray of Creation are distinct from the 'diagram of everything living,' which for the sake of simplicity, I have not described (see SM, p.323). Gurdjieff explains the differences between this diagram and the other two by claiming that this new diagram represents what serves as food for any specific level. The diagram is perhaps best regarded as an extension of the table of cosmoses, especially concerning the levels below the human. It includes one and two-brained beings or animals, plants, and it distinguishes between minerals and metals. This diagram of everything living is slightly different from Bennett's own adapted version, which he calls the diagram of 'essence classes' (Bennett, 1973, p.205).

5
Metaphysics

'Metaphysics' means beyond physics. It is the study of questions concerning the fundamental nature of the universe, such as 'Does the universe consists only of matter?' 'Does God exist?' which cannot be answered by experimental physics alone. In Gurdjieff's system, the deep metaphysical questions, such as those pertaining to the existence of God, the problem of evil and the meaning of life, are answered by showing how the development of human potential fits into the cosmic scheme described in the previous chapter.

Creation

The Common Father Endlessness (World 1) manifests Itself in space, through the internal action called the Autoegogratic process, as the Holy Sun Absolute of World 3 and the formless ether-like Etherokilno (Bel, p.748). This is the first step of creation. However, the Sun Absolute and the formless Etherokilno could not remain in a state of static equilibrium because of the effect of the 'Merciless Heropass,' or time. Time has a destructive entropic effect and, as a result, the volume of the Sun Absolute began to diminish (Bel, p. 749).

To counteract this, the Sun Absolute (or God as World 3) willed the Theomertmalogos (the Word-God), or a creative energy, that reacted with the all-pervasive Etherokilno to form the Megalocosmos, or our living universe (Bel, p.756-7). This was the second step of creation. This living universe maintains itself and the Sun Absolute through the process of reciprocal maintenance or Trogoautoegocrat (Bel, p.789). In other words, each level of being produces the energies that are necessary

41

for the maintenance of the others above and below it. In brief, God created the universe in order that He should not die.

In this way, creation continuously unfolds through a process of energy interchanges that constitute the involution of the universe, through the descending octaves that comprise the many rays of creation, one of which is ours. At the same time, the universe evolves through the energy exchanges of the various ascending octaves of each ray, which maintain the Sun Absolute against the effects of time. In this way, the created universe is like the breathing in and out of World 3.

This dynamic equilibrium maintains itself through the action of the two fundamental laws, the laws of three and seven described in the previous chapter. For instance, the law of three states that 'the higher blends with the lower in order to actualize the middle' (Bel, p.751). In the case of creation, the Theomertmalogos vitalizes the formless Etherokilno to create the Megalocomsos.

Space and Time

Gurdjieff claims that the fixed relations between the cosmoses can be represented as the relation between zero and infinity (SM, p.206). This means that, for each cosmos, the one above it represents a higher spatio-temporal dimension. Because each cosmos has a real physical existence, it views itself as consisting of three-dimensional bodies (SM, p.206). In other words, from the point of view of World 48, World 24 is analogous to four-dimensional space. (Gurdjieff also suggests that each cosmos must regard itself as a four dimensionally extended in time, but this is a complication which I shall ignore (SM, p.215)).

Gurdjieff states that there are only seven dimensions, from six to zero. The sixth dimension represents all possibilities co-existing as actual. The fifth dimension designates the eternal existence of possibilities. The fourth dimension stands for the sequence of actualization of individual possibilities, one by one (i.e. linear time). The third consists of volumes; the second, planes; the first, lines and finally, the zero-dimension consists of dimensionless points (SM, p.211).

From our point of view, taking World 48 as three dimensional, World 6 would be six dimensional. This means that all the possibilities of our world are realized at the level of the Milky Way galaxy (World 6). Conversely, from the point of view of World 6 (taking itself as three-dimensional), our earthly life constitutes a section of a section of a section of reality. From the perspective of World 6, we in World 48 are as unreal or incomplete as a dimensionless point. On the other hand, from the perspective of World 1, World 6 is only as real as a one-dimensional line.

Gurdjieff also claims that each cosmos has a different scale of time (Bel, p.125). Ouspensky reports Gurdjieff as affirming that the period of sleeping and waking of organic beings represents a period of breath for the biosphere (SM, p.213). Ouspensky himself uses this comment to construct a table of relative time periods. His idea is based on two principles. First, for each cosmos, the natural definition of time is constituted by four typical periods: 1) the normal duration of a life, 2) the duration of the sleeping and waking cycle, 3) the length of time of a breath and 4) the duration of the present moment of an impression. Second, what counts as a breath at one level will count as a day at the next higher level, and so on. In other words, a lifetime for us in World 48 (roughly 80 years), constitutes a day for World 24, a breath (or three seconds) for World 12, and the present moment of an impression for World 6 (or about $1/10,000^{th}$ of a second). In other words, the period of time that we perceive as 80 years would be merely one $1/10,000^{th}$ of a second for World 6.

In fact, the above explanation is a simplification, because Ouspensky actually applies his two principles to Gurdjieff's diagram of all living things, which we mentioned in the appendix of the previous chapter, rather than to the table of cosmoses. According to Ouspensky's calculations, the life of World 1 lasts 90 to the power of 28 years (SM, p. 332).

Gurdjieff himself dismissed Ouspensky's table of relative times as speculation (SM, p.329-41). However, Gurdjieff himself advances the general idea that time is perceived differently at each level of being (Bel. p.125-6). Finally, Ouspensky describes his table as representing the relativity of time. However, it seems more accurate to describe it as a table of the relativity of time perceptions. The idea is not the same as Einstein's claim that time is relative to velocity.

The Absolute

There are some differences between the picture of the Absolute as given by the early Gurdjieff reported in the works of Ouspensky, and the later descriptions given by Gurdjieff himself in *Beelzebub's Tales*. The later work describes the Absolute in more personal terms, such as 'our Common Father' and 'His All-Loving, Endlessly Merciful and Absolutely Just Creator Endlessness' (Bel, p.745). However, even in the earlier period, Gurdjieff refers to the Absolute as if it were a being with a will (FW p.194).

Despite the differences, the earlier and later conceptions of the Absolute have some striking similarities. First, the Absolute is not all-powerful. The Creator is not able to directly conquer the entropic effects of time. To overcome those effects, He has to create a self-maintaining universe. Furthermore, the Creator is not able to directly intervene in the workings of this universe, which is governed by a varying number of laws. His will creates the universe, which then unfolds according to a plan and the appropriate laws (Bel, p.756).

The will of the Absolute cannot directly express itself in the lower worlds, but it manifests itself only indirectly through the relevant inescapable natural laws appropriate to each level. Because the Absolute cannot intervene in our world, Gurdjieff rules out the conception of a miracle as a violation of all causal laws and as a direct divine intervention. Instead, what we consider to be a miracle is the manifestation in this world of one the laws of a higher world. For instance, there are 48 laws governing our world; but three of these laws apply to World 3. An event in our world that conforms to these three laws would appear to be a miracle (SM, p. 84).

Second, there is the strong suggestion in Gurdjieff's work that Absolute is not omniscient. The concept of the relativity of wholeness, explained in the previous chapter, implies that, from the point of view of higher levels, we do not even exist as individual beings. In the earlier period of his teachings, Gurdjieff explicitly claims that individual humans do not exist at all from the point of view of the universe as a whole (FW, p.201), and that the Absolute knows nothing of us humans (FW, p.215). The points regarding the dimensions and the relativity of time perceptions mentioned above reinforce these conclusions. In the later period, in *Beelzebub*, Gurdjieff represents those higher beings that are aware of our existence as being unable to understand the suffering and the conditions of our lives. For example, Gurdjieff claims that the deficiencies of our human situation, the events that might correspond to the 'fall of man' in the Christian tradition, are due to the errors of higher beings (Bennett, 1988, p.87).

The Cosmic Error

Due to an error of calculation, a vast comet called Kondoor struck the earth (Bel, p. 82). Two fragments flew of the earth, the moon and the smaller, and as yet undiscovered, Anulios, and threatened the stability of the solar system. As a result, the Common Father sent the archangel Sakaki to solve the problems. Sakaki decided that the moon and Anulios could be stabilized if they could be provided with an energy, called akokin, which is produced by the death of living organisms (Bel. p.84-5). Thus, Sakaki caused life to evolve on earth, so that akokin could be used to feed the moon.

After a long time, three-brain beings with the potential of attaining Objective Reason, or we humans, evolved on the earth. The Most High Commission, which included the archangel Looisos, was concerned that these beings would understand their true situation, and that they might revolt. So, they implanted in us humans the organ Kundabuffer, so that we would experience indiscriminate pleasure in a hypnotic, egoistic dream-state (Bel. p. 88-9). In this way, Looisos ensured that humans would blindly serve the developmental needs of the moon, at the cost of stunting our own potential.

To understand this story more fully, we must appreciate that, according to Gurdjieff, the moon, like other celestial bodies, is itself trying to develop, It is trying to reach the same level as the earth (Bel, p.181). For it reach that level, the earth itself would have to develop into a new sun. Gurdjieff said that

> The intelligence of the sun is divine. But the earth can become the same; only of course it is not guaranteed, and the earth may die having attained nothing (SM., p.25).

In this manner, in order for the moon to develop, a new solar system would have to be formed. A similar pattern of development may occur in the system of Jupiter. (Gurdjieff's idea was portrayed in Arthur Clarke's 2010, in which Jupiter becomes a new star and its satellites become planets).

To return to the main story, ironically, the organ Kundabuffer was later removed from humans, and our capacity to attain Objective Reason was thereby restored (Bel, p.90). Despite this restoration, the results of the organ Kundabuffer have stayed with us, leaving most people in an egoistic dream-like state, waiting to feed the moon after death. However, we are no longer condemned to such a state. We can escape this fate.

In the light of this story, we should modify the account of the role of organic life given in the previous chapter. Organic life is a huge accumulator of energy gathered from the sun and the rest of the solar system by the earth to feed itself and the development of the moon. At death, everything that lives releases energy, akokin, to the moon. Souls that go to the moon find themselves in the 'place of outer darkness' of the Christian tradition, where there is 'weeping and the gnashing of teeth' (SM, p.85). In other words, the choice between heaven and hell is the choice between feeding the sun or the moon (Gurdjieff, 1975, p.198). Our spiritual development consists in a struggle to become free form the mechanical influences of the moon (SM, p. 85 and p.305-6). This last point must be contrasted with Gurdjieff's later claim in *Beelzebub's Tales* that Heaven and Hell should not be thought of as places (Bel, p. 804).

How should we understand this story? Does Gurdjieff intend it literally or as an allegory? It might be an allegory for the psychological history of humanity. For example, Orage suggests that the comet Kondoor may represent puberty, and the moon, the lunatic aspect of the unconscious (Moore, p.49). On the other hand, Bennett interprets at least parts of Gurdjieff's story literally. He contends that very early humans had erect backs and possibly a form of intelligence much like modern Homo Sapiens. Neanderthal man, on the other hand, had a curved spine and might correspond to humans with the organ Kundabuffer implanted. About 35,000 years ago, Neanderthals were replaced by the precursors of contemporary Homo Sapiens and this might correspond to the removal of the organ Kundabuffer. In other words, according to Bennett, human evolution stood still for about a hundred thousand years during the time the organ Kundabuffer was present within us (Bennett, 1973, p.251).

The Meaning of Life

In light of the above, we can understand Gurdjieff's tale of a rich magician who owned many sheep. In order to prevent them from wandering off, the magician hypnotized his flock and suggested to them that they were immortal, that he was a good master who loved them dearly and that they were not sheep at all, but lions and humans. In this way, the sheep quietly awaited their death and skinning (SM, p.219). In a sense, the purpose of our lives is to not die like sheep.

Contemporary science studies the mechanisms that govern the universe and life as a machine without addressing their purpose. Rather than rejecting the questions 'What is the purpose of the universe?' and 'What is the purpose of life?' Gurdjieff tries to answer them.

In Gurdjieff's system, in general the meaning of life is its purpose. As the universe unfolds along its various rays or branches, energy in its finer forms has to be converted into denser forms. Organic life performs that conversion by transforming sunlight into matter and by producing the energy akokin. Organic life is a means to feed the development of the earth and moon. It fulfills its meaning or function without intending to. In Gurdjieff's system, the created universe itself has a meaning or purpose. Our Father Endlessness or World 1 manifests itself as the Sun Absolute or World 3 but, in so doing, it becomes subject to the ravages of time. To counteract the otherwise inevitable destructive effect of time, the Sun Absolute creates a living universe from which energy flows out and back to the Sun Absolute through the process of reciprocal maintenance.

What is the meaning of human life? Once again, it serves various cosmic purposes. However, unlike the rest of organic life on earth, human life not only serves the natural involutionary process by which energy becomes denser, but it can also serve the almost unnatural evolutionary process whereby coarser energies become transformed into finer ones. In other words, we can serve the universe's evolution as well as its involution. This requires learning to swim against the current.

In *Beelzebub's Tales* (p.130-1), Gurdjieff distinguishes two principles of human life. The first, called 'Foolasnitamnian,' requires the development of a will through conscious work and intentional suffering and, thereby, involves the growth of the kesdjan body. The second, called 'Itoklanoz,' consists in the fragmentation of the will into opposing likes and dislikes. The fate of human beings after the death of the physical body depends on this difference. For persons without a kesdjan body, death is simply the release of akokin energy for the sake of the moon, as it is for all other forms of organic life. In contrast, persons with a kesdjan body can survive the death of their physical bodies.

In the light of these claims, we can affirm that, in Gurdjieff's system, the meaning of human existence consists in three major purposes (for comments on this kind of idea, see Thomson, 2002). The first is our personal concern with our own mortality. The second, due to our position in the general scheme of the cosmoses, is to provide the appropriate energies for the development of the earth and moon. This aspect of the meaning of our lives does not depend at all on what we do. We fulfill this purpose at death, when these energies are released. The third purpose is to provide higher energies for higher cosmoses. This requires struggling against the flow of nature. We can only fulfill this purpose by struggling against the sleep-inducing and mechanical effects of the organ Kundabuffer, and by acquiring the finer bodies, which are needed for higher states of consciousness. In this way, the first and third purposes of human life are different facets of the same process of evolution (Bel, p.144).

6
Religion

A person will be most interested in the work if he or she is disappointed in his or her religion. This does not mean that the person should lose his or her faith, but rather that he or she feels disappointment that its teachings and methods do not lead to results (SM, p.243). The same point applies to science and philosophy. Being disappointed in science does not mean losing interest in the systematic acquisition of knowledge, but rather in understanding its limitations.

Traditional Theology

Gurdjieff's cosmological metaphysics contradicts traditional monotheistic theology in two fundamental ways. These points of conflict have already been mentioned, but let us briefly review them.

The Absolute

As mentioned earlier, Gurdjieff's conception of the Absolute changed between the early period as reported by Ouspensky and the later period of Gurdjieff's own writings. However, in both phases, his conception of the Absolute differs from the traditional monotheistic conception of God. Primarily, the Absolute is neither all-powerful nor all-knowing.

Is the Absolute God? In Gurdjieff's system, the Absolute has no direct relation to us and cannot be conceived as a personal God. Furthermore, the hierarchy of Being, or the principle of the relativity of wholeness, suggests that the idea of the divine is itself relative to the levels concerned. In other words, World 24 is already divine for we humans, who inhabit World 48. Gurdjieff expresses the same point from another point of view, by claiming that 'the Absolute is God for gods' (FW, p.408).

In *Beelzebub*, Gurdjieff ridicules the way most people understand the Biblical saying that God created humans in His own image. Gurdjieff claims that God is often portrayed as a man, specifically as an old gentleman with a beard (Bel, 776-7). Instead, the Biblical saying should be understood in terms of the table of cosmoses and the idea that all levels of existence are governed by the same two fundamental laws (Bel, p. 778-80). Gurdjieff expresses this with the saying; 'As above, so below.'

Immortality

The monotheistic religions (Judaism, Christianity and Islam) claim that humans have an immortal soul. In contrast, Gurdjieff's teaching is that we humans have nothing resembling a soul unless we acquire one through conscious effort and intentional suffering. However, the 'soul' that we can acquire consists of bodies of different degrees of materiality, which can permeate and survive this earthly body (Gurdjieff, 1975, p.201). Furthermore, these higher bodies are not strictly speaking immortal in the sense of being everlasting. Even World 3 cannot escape the ravages of time (SM, p.91).

Relativity of Religion

Religion manifests itself in different ways at different levels, because the way a person understands religion must be suitable for his or her level of being. Thus, the religion of a person number 1 will be quite different from that of person number 5. There are higher and lower ways of understanding religion.

Similar points apply to the practice of prayer. Prayer at level 1, 2, and 3 is a form of self-consolation (SM, p.300). Prayers can also be petitions. Ouspensky says 'Turgenev wrote somewhere that all our ordinary prayers can be reduced to one: 'Lord, make it so that twice two be not four'' (SM, p.95). However, prayer can also be a means for self-observation and self-remembering, especially when we reflect on the meaning of the words involved (SM, p.301). For instance, Gurdjieff claims that when we attend to the way we say the word 'I,' the sound can appear in different parts of the body, such as in the head and the chest, and even outside the body (Gurdjieff, 1975, p.234). This was an exercise for feeling the different centers practiced in the monasteries of Mount Athos (TS, p.134; SM, p. 304).

Gurdjieff also mentions how the original teachings of the religions have been lost through time. Originally, the Christian church was a school in which the various rites and ceremonies had specific meanings and purposes, which have now been lost (SM, p.96 and p.302). The Gospels were originally written for the followers of Christ, who already had understanding and, as a consequence, much of their original meaning has been lost. For example, in the Gospels there are several allusions to the necessity of awaking dying and being born. Gurdjieff understands these sayings in terms of a three step process, summarized in the sentence: 'If a person dies without having awakened, he or she cannot be born' (SM, p. 217). 'Being born' refers to the birth of an indivisible self and 'dying' refers to becoming free from our normal petty attachments. The story in the Gospels of Christ's disciples sleeping while he prayed in the Garden of Gethsemane relates their inner state at the time (SM, p.144).

The *Psychological Commentaries* of Maurice Nicoll contain many interpretations of the Christian religion in light of Gurdjieff's system. His books, *The New Man*, and *The Mark*, contain similar interpretations of the parables of the Gospels. A parable is a medium of connecting higher and lower meanings in which material objects can represent higher meaning. Consider, for example, this Biblical quote: 'The Disciples of Christ were sent out to preach the Gospels without shoes' (Matthew, X, 10), According to Nicoll, shoes and feet signify the sensual part of a person because they touch the earth. This idea also helps explain the meaning of those rituals in which a person must remove his or her shoes before entering a holy place, and also the significance of Christ's washing his disciples feet (Nicoll, 1954, p.3-7).

As another example, consider also the following. In Matthew XIII, we are told that Jesus spoke in parables to the multitudes on the beach from a boat on the sea. This represents the idea that Jesus was on a different level of being from the earth. One of these parables is that of the sower who sowed seeds, some of which fell by the way side and were devoured by birds. The seeds represent the higher teaching present within a person and the birds represent thoughts. Some of the seeds were also trodden underfoot. The allusion to feet was mentioned earlier Nicoll, 1954, p. 61-4).

One of Gurdjieff's own most surprising reinterpretations of the New Testament concerns the role of Judas, who did not betray Christ, but rather permitted him to accomplish his mission, and who was Christ's most devoted follower (Bel, p.739-42; Bennett, 1975, p.262). This idea was vividly portrayed in Kazantzakis' novel, *The Last Temptation of Christ*.

In *Beelzebub*, Gurdjieff describes how the teachings of the Buddha also were altered through misunderstanding. Originally, part of the Buddha's teaching was that his followers should make conscious efforts to bear the unpleasant manifestations of other people, an idea that was lost when his followers retreated to monasteries (Bel, p.242-3). He also describes how the idea of the organ Kundabuffer became perverted into the concept of Kundali (Bel, p.249-50). As a consequence, Kundali, which is really a source of the energy of imagination, became the spiritual basis of some Indian teachings.

Christian Morality

Despite the above criticisms, Christianity was important for Gurdjieff. During his early searches, he visited Jerusalem, the monasteries of Mount Athos, and the Coptic Church in Abyssinia. Moore describes how Gurdjieff taught his first foreign pupil, the pianist, Sir Paul Dukes how to sing the Lord's Prayer on a single even breath in a rich 'bass note about G2 below middle C' (Moore, p.75). Dukes later wrote that Gurdjieff had made the Gospels 'intensely personal' (Moore, p.76). One of the sayings placed on the wall of the study house of the Prieuré was 'Respect all religions' (Gurdjieff, 1975, p.274).

Gurdjieff also said that the aim of the Institute was to help people become real Christians. This, he said, is not easy. For example, Christ enjoins one to love one's neighbors as oneself, but in our present state, we cannot will ourselves to love. First, we have to become able to do this, and only then, one can follow the commandments. Otherwise, we are Christians in name only (Bennett, 1973, p.143-5). A Christian is a person 'who is able to fulfill the Commandments' (Gurdjieff, 1975, p.154). In our present state, we are incapable of turning the other cheek. We are machines, and the practice of Christian morality requires that we able to be responsible for ourselves (SM, p.102 and 157). To understand this point better, let us turn to Gurdjieff's views of morality.

7

Morality

Gurdjieff claims that, strictly speaking, morality is impossible for us. Human beings are machines, and morality is not possible for machines (Gurdjieff, 1975, p.77; SM p.349). Thus, it is useless to assert that humans ought to do this or should not do that, because machines do not have a will (SM, p.255). In this way, our ordinary conception of morality makes an assumption that is false, namely that we are free to choose our actions and feelings.

In addition, we shall see in this chapter that Gurdjieff gives a powerful three pronged critique of the practice of everyday social morality. First, normally morality consists of no more than social demands, which are entirely subjective and thus often have no real value. Second, our feelings of moral blame, indignation and injustice are usually no more than expressions of dislike based on a false egoism, on a form of identification, which Gurdjieff calls internal consideration. Thirdly, because of this identification, ordinary morality actually hinders our progress towards feeling real conscience and becoming really moral. It is part of what keeps us asleep.

Gurdjieff's contrast between ordinary and true morality bears some similarities to Nietzsche's (1844-1900) distinction between slave and master morality. Both give moral critiques of our normal understanding and practice of morality; both claim that moralizing is immoral. It keeps us asleep as sheep. However, Nietzsche and Gurdjieff diverge in their understanding of true morality, as we shall presently see.

Conscience

According to Gurdjieff, what we in society customarily call morality is purely subjective and artificial. It is not really morality at all. It consists of various taboos, restrictions and social demands that vary from culture to culture (Bel, p.343; SM, p.156-7).

These demands generate buffers that prevent us from feeling the contradictory nature of our many personalities. In other words, these restrictions and demands encourage us to compartmentalize our lives and lie to ourselves. They so encourage us because morality involves individuals identifying themselves with their feelings, such as indignation. The buffers that are generated in this way have the effect of putting real conscience to sleep. Through the effect of these buffers, an individual can feel that he or she is always right, and thus, the buffers prevent us from feeling the real morality of conscience (SM p.154-5).

In this way, Gurdjieff contrasts ordinary subjective morality with objective conscience. Whereas the taboos and expectations that constitute ordinary morality vary from place to place, one conscience can never contradict another (SM, p.157). Conscience is the same for all persons.

In our state of deep hypnotic sleep, conscience does not function. What we call conscience is simply the buffers or compartment walls that permit us to lie to ourselves. In sharp contrast, real conscience involves feeling with the emotional center the truth regarding a specific subject (FW, p.152). It is the state in which a person cannot hide anything from him or herself. Conscience is the manifestation of real consciousness in the feelings. Higher consciousness involves being immediately aware of oneself and of everything we know about something (FW, p.151). Conscience is to the feelings what consciousness is to the mind. If a person felt conscience, then the individual would be able to be aware of all the contradictory emotions that he or she feels at that time regarding a particular thing. Such a state would be almost unbearable because a person would feel the 'shame and the horror of it all.' For this reason, we opt to allow our conscience to be put to sleep (SM, p.154).

However, a person who permits and cultivates the temporary awakening of the conscience through self-remembering will gradually feel a 'very subtle joy,' despite the initial suffering and shame (SM, 156). As a result, the person will no longer be able to deceive him or herself as before (SM, p.245). This is reminiscent of one of the sayings of Gurdjieff's father, 'Truth is that from which conscience can be at peace' (MRM, p.46).

True Consideration

As well as identifying ourselves with our psychological states, such as moods, we can identify ourselves in various ways with other people. Gurdjieff calls this 'internal considering.' For example, we often identify ourselves with what others think of us. In this mode, we complain when we feel that others are not sufficiently polite or respectful towards us. As a result of this, we hypocritically judge the actions of others in terms of their consequences and assess our own actions in terms of our own good intentions. As an antidote to this double standard, we can remember that nobody does anything deliberately for the sake of evil. Everybody acts in the interests of the good, as he or she understands it (SM, p.158).

Another form of internal considering occurs when we identify ourselves with conditions that displease us, such as the behavior of another person. This type of considering is often the cause of the judgment that those conditions are unjust. The resulting feelings of indignation prevent us from seeing this as a form of identification. People can even have such feelings of 'injustice' towards impersonal conditions, such as the weather (SM, p.151).

A similar form of consideration or identification occurs when a person feels that he or she is not another person into account sufficiently. The subsequent feelings of guilt may lead the person to judge that he or she ought to do so and so, but such judgments are only a mechanical expression of internal considering or identification (FW, p.128). Such forms of identification prevent us from being conscious, and consciousness is necessary for the real consideration of others.

In contrast with these forms of internal consideration, there is the external considering of other people, which requires putting oneself in the position of the other person and taking his or her requirements into account, rather than one's own. One of the sayings on the wall of the Prieuré study house was 'Only he who can be just who can enter into the position of others' (Gurdjieff, 1975, p.275).

External considering is hard to attain because, first, it requires considerable understanding of other people. Such understanding is difficult to achieve because the functioning of our centers is mixed up. We try to appreciate the feelings of other people with the intellect. In this sense, 'a full man does not understand a hungry one' (SM, p.110). Second, external considering is difficult because it requires both control over oneself and the act of self-remembering, for otherwise it will turn into a form of internal considering. Unlike internal considering, external considering is not mechanical (FW, p.129). External considering is a necessary ingredient of the work on oneself, because it is an expression of the extent to which we value the work (SM, p.154).

Another saying placed on the wall of the study hall in the Prieuré was 'The best means of obtaining felicity in life is the ability to consider externally always, internally never' (Gurdjieff, 1975, p.274). In short, happiness consists in caring for others. However, in sharp contrast, Gurdjieff also writes:

> In order to be in reality a really just and good altruist, it is inevitably required first of all to be an out and out egoist (Bel, p.1236).

By 'egoism,' Gurdjieff does not mean normal vanity and self-love, which occupy almost half of our time (Gurdjieff, 1975, p.267-9). Rather, he means the ability to be free of them. In other words, to care for others it is necessary to care for oneself. This is because genuine altruism, or external consideration, is not possible for a machine. It is first necessary to become master of oneself. In summary, false egoism generates false altruism, and true altruism requires true egoism. False egoism and altruism both consist in identifying oneself. True egoism consists in freeing oneself from such identification, and true altruism requires that freedom.

Earlier I drew some comparisons between Gurdjieff and Nietzsche's view of morality. In particular, both condemn the morality of the herd as enslaving and insist on a transvaluation of human values. Both emphasize 'self-overcoming,' to use Nietzsche's phrase, and the need for will. Aside from their very different views of metaphysics and truth, a crucial point of divergence is that, for Nietzsche, the process of transformation consists in overcoming the ascetic ideals inherent in modern religious culture. In contrast, Gurdjieff's teaching retains some aspects of those ideals, such as altruism, sacrifice and idea of higher powers. Whereas Gurdjieff emphasizes the need for a transformation of religion, Nietzsche insists on its end.

Beyond Good and Evil

Dualistic thought conceives morality in terms of the conflict between good and evil. Given the primordial nature of the law of three, Gurdjieff considers this a fundamental and harmful misunderstanding of morality, which cannot lead to results. Because of our third force blindness, we identify good and evil in terms of our likes and dislikes or feelings of approval and disapproval (Bennett, 1978, p. 31-2). In these ways, the concepts of good and evil are actually impediments to the process of self-perfection (Bel, p.1126).

What does replacing the good/evil dichotomy with a triad consist in? It consists in no longer opposing an unattainable ideal with an undesirable reality in such a way that makes progress impossible. It consists in looking for the third reconciling force that brings a new understanding of the situation, which allows the otherwise unattainable objective to be achieved without compromise (Bennett, 1978, p.34-7). For example, the ideal of changing the world becomes replaced by the objective of transforming oneself through the understanding that one is asleep.

Given this view of morality, there is no need for the concept of evil as such (SM p.227). People always act for the good as they perceive and understand it. Harm results from the fact that our understanding is so limited, which in turn is a consequence of the fact that we are sleeping machines. Furthermore, according to the tales of Beelzebub, our sleeping condition is ultimately due to the limitations of higher beings, which result from their inevitable lack of understanding of our condition, which is itself a consequence of the nature of the different levels of being. In brief, it is inevitable that the natural world cannot have the perfection of World 1 (see pages 44-45).

Conclusion

According to Gurdjieff, morality requires one to work on oneself in the ways described in Chapters 3 and 4. To be able to follow the dictates of conscience and to be able to really love one's neighbor, we need to be free of our mechanical sleep like state. This requires a process of self-transformation.

Contrast this view with the popular understanding of morality that is framed entirely in terms of public policy and social issues, such as euthanasia and the death penalty. With Gurdjieff, the desire to change the world becomes converted to the need to transform oneself. Morality is more of a way to free oneself of one's own likes and dislikes rather than a way to impose them on others. This is fundamentally because morality and caring for others cannot be mechanical.

For this reason, according to Gurdjieff, morality requires us to not identify ourselves with our feelings, by not saying 'I' to them (N1, p.62). By paying attention to our emotions in the right way, we can begin to separate ourselves from them, and thereby begin to acquire a self that is distinct from them, which will eventually permit us to will freely and, thereby, be able to follow the dictates of conscience.

8
Epistemology

A theoretical study of Gurdjieff's system should not ignore epistemology, the theory of knowledge. On the one hand, many readers will ask 'On what evidential basis does Gurdjieff make his various psychological and metaphysical claims?' On the other hand, although Gurdjieff has little to say directly about epistemology as such, there are several epistemological claims inherent in his work. Gurdjieff's system is based on four major epistemological assumptions.

The Need for Verification

The first principle is that no claim to knowledge of the system should be based on pure faith (SM, p.228). Gurdjieff's claims need to be based on verification and not faith. Ouspensky reports that

> There is no question of faith or belief in all this. Quite the opposite, the system teaches people to believe in absolutely nothing. You must verify everything that you see, hear and feel. Only in that way can you come to something (FW, p. 6).

As we saw in Chapter 3, the Fourth Way depends on understanding rather than faith. The word 'faith' here means believing something without having any evidence. In contrast, understanding requires us to verify the claims of the Gurdjieffian system for ourselves. Gurdjieff also asserts that, for almost everything a person claims to know, there are methods for verifying. As an example of this attitude, when Gurdjieff spoke about the possibility of a universal language, a student asked whether this was the same phenomenon described in the Acts as the action of the Holy Ghost. Ouspensky reports:

> I noticed that such questions always irritated Gurdjieff. "I don't know. I wasn't there," he said (SM, p.96).

When asked whether Christ taught dances, Gurdjieff replied, "I was not there to see" (Gurdjieff, 1975, p.86). This aspect of Gurdjieff's teaching makes it quite different from the traditional monotheistic religions, which ultimately rely on some kind of faith, and which do not enjoin their adherents to believe only what they can verify.

The Study of Awareness

The second Gurdjieffian epistemological principle specifies the basis for this verification. Knowledge claims must be based on direct experiential evidence, and in particular the evidence of self-observation and self-remembering. In other words, verification must begin with observation of oneself, and it is necessarily first personal. For example, the workings of the different centers have different phenomenological or experiential flavors or tastes with which one can become directly acquainted (SM, p.117). For example, one can only discover for oneself whether different states of consciousness are possible. Behind this general idea is the assumption that one can *know* consciousness directly only in oneself (SM, p.116).

Through the work as described in Chapter 3, Gurdjieff defines forms of acquiring psychological self-knowledge that are essentially different from behaviorism, psycho-analysis and Cartesian introspection, which were the dominant psychological paradigms of the time. Gurdjieff's system is different from behaviorism because it advocates direct study of one's own psychological states, including one's attention, rather than studying input-output relations or the behavior of experimental subjects. It differs from psychoanalysis because it does not involve the study of the unconscious.

Finally, it is different from Descartes' (1596–1650) notion of introspection for three reasons. First, Gurdjieff's self-remembering requires dividing the attention and, thus, it is not a question of attending to the content of mental states in the way that knowledge through introspection does. Self-remembering is not attending to experience as such, but rather to the way in which one experiences. It involves attending to one's attention, and thereby separating oneself from one's moods, thoughts and feelings.

Second, Gurdjieff's self-observation has a wider scope of application than pure introspection. It requires one to attend to one's postures and bodily movements, as well as to one's mental and emotional states. Furthermore, it requires one to make experiments in self-observation, or to observe oneself in both unusual and typical situations. One can attend to the full workings of the human machine only by varying one's circumstances or the conditions of observation. For example, it requires self-observation while performing the movements and other exercises.

Third, Gurdjieff's explanation of self-observation essentially involves a conceptual framework that is alien to Descartes' introspection. For example, it requires the concepts of the various centers, of an individual's chief fault, and of a person as a sleeping machine. In this way, it is more theory and value laden than introspection. Furthermore, it involves factual judgments about oneself. There is a fundamental difference between the report 'I feel as if I am asleep' and the factual assertion 'I have noticed that I am asleep.' The latter makes the claim that one really is asleep, which the former lacks. With pure introspection, one simply reports the content of one's experiences.

Phenomenology

In some ways, these aspects of Gurdjieff's teaching are similar to phenomenology. Edmund Husserl (1859-1938) developed the phenomenological method to provide knowledge of experience and the a priori structure of intentional states, which opposes the encroachment of the naturalism of contemporary science into the psychological field. According to Husserl, mental states are intentional because they are directed to things in the world and have a meaning or content. This point distinguishes the mental and physical and permits the study and description of mental states without any ontological presuppositions concerning what exists. Husserl's phenomenological method consists in directing the attention exclusively to the content of experience, rather than to the external object of the experience or to matters of fact. It is the study of intentional experience as such.

Despite the similarities, there are fundamental differences between phenomenology and Gurdjieff's concept of self-observation. These differences amount to the fact that the two have very different aims. Phenomenology attempts to study experience as such and, for this reason, it attempts to bracket or suspend all ontological presuppositions about the natural world. In contrast, the aim of Gurdjieff's self-observation is to acquaint the person with those aspects of everyday experience that point towards the possibility of, and the need for, self-development, and the aim of self-remembering is to awaken higher states of consciousness in the person.

From Psychology to Cosmology

Let us return to the second general epistemological principle that knowledge of Gurdjieff's system must be based on direct experiential evidence. This seems to be a reasonable principle concerning some of the psychological aspects of the system (apart from the qualifications mentioned below). But how does the second principle apply to the cosmology? One simple answer is that it does not, and that is one reason why Gurdjieff tended to concentrate more on the practical aspects of the work, which his students could experience for themselves, especially in the later periods.

However, Gurdjieff provides a different answer. For example, he claims that his students should become familiar the working of the laws of three and seven within themselves before looking for instances of it in external events (SM, p.135). Bennett says that we must acquire a taste of the law from the inside, by experiencing the quality of each stage, rather than theoretically studying external applications of the law (Bennett 1988, p. 97-100). In *Beelzebub*, Gurdjieff says that examples of the three forces of the law of three 'may be discovered in all manifestations of our psychic life' (SM, p.78). Here is another example: when Ouspensky was speculating about the law of three, Gurdjieff said to him: "That is a very long way away yet... Better to think of yourself; of your work" (SM, p. 264). The implication of this statement is that, later on with sufficient effort, Ouspensky would be able to verify for himself the truth of his speculations.

Perhaps, similar claims could be made for other aspects of Gurdjieff's cosmology. For example, perhaps persons with a higher state of consciousness can discern and distinguish the effects of higher energies upon their psychological states and thereby indirectly have evidence for his aspect of the cosmology. In *Beelzebub*, Gurdjieff coins the term 'Ooletesnokhian sight' for the capacity to directly perceive finer forms of matter (Bel, p.304). This idea brings us to the third general epistemological principle inherent in Gurdjieff's system.

The Knowledge of Higher States

The third epistemological principle is that there are certain facts that people can know directly only when they have reached a higher level of consciousness. Phenomena transcending the categories of ordinary everyday things cannot be observed in an ordinary state of consciousness. They require higher states of awareness (SM, p.256). For example, experiential knowledge of the unity of everything can only be attained with objective consciousness (SM, p.279). We can only have knowledge of finer forms of energy in higher states of consciousness. This general point has three implications.

1) This third principle indicates a qualification on the scope of the first two. It means that Gurdjieff's cosmology and some of his psychology is beyond us in the sense that we cannot experientially verify such claims unless we acquire higher states of consciousness.

2) This third principle also means that one must know what one can and cannot know directly (FW, p.7). In other words, this principle requires us to distinguish between claims that one can know in the ordinary state of consciousness and those that one cannot.

3) The third principle also leads to Gurdjieff's distinction between knowing and being.

Knowing and Being

The knowledge a person can acquire depends on his or her being (Bel, p.394; SM p. 65). If knowledge advances beyond the level of being of the subject, then it will become theoretical, inapplicable to everyday life, and unsuited to the person's being. For example, it will become knowledge of a detail without understanding of the whole, or knowledge of form without that of essence (SM, p. 65). For a person who is asleep, there is no practical difference between knowledge and ignorance of the different levels of being. Ouspensky reports that Gurdjieff warned his pupils of the dangers of too much theorizing especially with regard to his cosmological system and, in particular, the law of octaves (SM, p.135). He says:

Change of knowledge comes from change of being. Knowledge in itself is nothing (Gurdjieff, 1975, p. 79)

Gurdjieff uses this idea of knowledge depending on being to distinguish knowing and understanding (SM, p. 67). Understanding does not mean the same as knowing. A person can have much knowledge without understanding what he or she knows by failing to appreciate that the implications of the knowledge. For this reason, increasing knowledge does not automatically increase understanding. Most people recognize this distinction in application to their everyday lives; they see that knowing something theoretically is not sufficient for real understanding, which involves knowing how to apply such knowledge. Gurdjieff expresses the difference between knowing and understanding in terms of the functioning of the centers. Whereas knowledge is the function of only one center, understanding is necessarily the function of all three centers: thinking, feeling and sensing.

Hypothetical Verification

The third epistemological principle might be understood as an appeal to the concept of the hypothetical verification of a knowledge claim. This is an idea that is sometimes employed in the philosophy of religion. Let us see how it can be applied in the Christian tradition. For example, during the life of our earthly body, we cannot verify the claims that the soul will survive death and that God exists. However, given that these claims are true, we will be able to verify them personally after the death of the body. At that time, we will know directly that God and the soul exist. Thus, although such claims to knowledge cannot be supported by direct experience now, they can be supported by appeal to certain future hypothetical observations. We may be able to verify them after the death of the body. However, the concept of such hypothetical verification in the philosophy of religion is contentious because it depends on the truth of the very claims in question.

In relation to Gurdjieff's system, one might argue that knowledge claims can be subject to a similar form of hypothetical verification, because they can be verified once one has achieved greater degrees of self-perfection. However, this idea is open to the same objection, namely that it presupposes the very claims under consideration.

Indirect Higher Knowledge

Implicit in Gurdjieff's system, there is a fourth general epistemological principle, namely that one can have indirect knowledge based on the higher direct knowledge of others (FW, p.109). This fourth principle supplements the third. We cannot acquire 'higher' knowledge directly because of our sleeping state of awareness, but the idea now is that we can acquire such knowledge indirectly because someone else knew or knows it directly.

Let us examine this fourth principle more carefully. How did Gurdjieff acquire this system of alleged cosmological knowledge? He claims that the cosmology and metaphysics of his system is part of the teachings known to different ancient schools. He discovered the elements of his system in the various journeys of his youth by studying with the teachers of these ancient traditions. This answer invites the question: 'How did those teachers acquire this knowledge?' They, or someone else, and perhaps Gurdjieff himself, must have acquired such knowledge directly. In other words, according to this idea, groups in the past knew these metaphysical claims directly from experience because they were in higher states of consciousness, and they passed down their knowledge to others, and thus indirectly to us.

Evaluation

I would like now to briefly critically evaluate these four epistemological principles. The purpose of this evaluation is not to show that certain aspects of Gurdjieff's system are false, but rather to present some challenges to the claim that they can be *known* to be true, even supposing that they are true.

The First Principle

The first epistemological principle is that the system needs to be verified rather than accepted on faith. This principle needs to be placed in context. Gurdjieff's epistemology is directed primarily to the needs of the work rather than to the requirements of epistemological values as such. Thus, when he affirms that no faith is required, he means that it is better for self-development that the individual verifies the teachings (SM, p.228). Faith in such matters runs contrary to the values inherent in the teaching. Understanding requires work: one should not wait for roasted pigeons to fly into one's mouth (Gurdjieff, 1975, p.28). Gurdjieff is not primarily concerned with the philosophical question whether, or under what conditions, certain beliefs might count as knowledge, which is the traditional problem of epistemology.

In other words, there are two issues at hand, which we should not conflate. First, there are the concerns of traditional epistemology, which can be seen as a set of epistemological value judgements and definitions. Primary amongst these might be the following:

1) Knowledge requires true belief supported by reasonable evidence
2) We should not believe claims that do not have some reasonable evidential support.
3) We should disbelieve claims that have evidence against them
4) We should neither believe nor disbelieve claims that have no reasonable evidence for or against them.

For the moment, I shall leave aside the vexed question of what counts as 'reasonable' evidence.

Second, there is Gurdjieff's concern that persons who work on themselves should have a healthy skepticism towards the teaching because that will motivate them to seek the direct experience that is necessary for their development. These two concerns are different because the first appeals directly to epistemological values and the second to the values of self-development. The importance of this difference will become apparent shortly.

The Second Principle

Gurdjieff's second epistemological principle is not as straightforward as it may first appear. For example, Gurdjieff claims that the process of realizing that is one asleep requires that one be convinced that one is asleep. This claim generates a problem. As Gurdjieff repeatedly points out, we humans are very suggestible and prone to self-deception. Thus, if one is convinced that one is asleep, and one observes carefully one's actions and psychological states given that conviction or presupposition, then one will probably find exactly what one expects to find. For this reason, self-observation is not sufficient on its own to generate knowledge claims, such as the affirmation that one is a sleeping machine. Notice that the relevant assertion is not that one feels like sleeping machine, but rather that one is one.

For this reason, the claim that the results of self-observation are repeatable is not sufficient to establish that they count as knowledge. Repeatability is necessary, but to count as knowledge, such results would also require some form of control. The point is not that Gurdjieff should have performed scientifically controlled experiments to test his methods, but rather that the second epistemological principle is subject to an important limitation.

To make this point vivid, we might contrast Gurdjieff's self-observation with the claims of certain forms of existentialist psychotherapy that stress that a person is defined by the choices that he or she makes. According to this idea, a person is largely constituted by the choices he or she makes. We live inauthentically when we deny that what we are is a result of our choices, for example by blaming external circumstances. By coming to realize this, we thereby recover responsibility for ourselves and allow ourselves to actively choose. Obviously, this form of existentialist therapy involves a principle that is denied by Gurdjieff, namely that the person has the capacity to choose. The epistemological problem is that, once a person presupposes that he or she does have that existential capacity for free choice, then the individual will certainly begin to 'perceive' the different choices that he or she has made. In other words, the presupposition affects perception. Similarly, Gurdjieff's claim that we are sleeping machines is subject to the same limitation. Similar points can be made about the psychological application of the laws of three and seven.

Nevertheless, in defense of the second principle, Gurdjieff insists that we should come to observe ourselves as we truly are, without self-deception, imagination and wishful thinking. Furthermore, in terms of aims of the system, the claim that one needs to be convinced that one is asleep makes some sense. First, it is necessary to counter-act the strong tendency to assume that one is not asleep. Second, Gurdjieff claims that it is sometimes possible for a person to enter into a state akin to self-remembering as it were by accident. However, such naturally occurring states have no real value because the subject does not understand their significance. In other words, self-remembering without the appropriate concepts is blind. The idea of concept-free self-observation does not make sense. Any kind of self-observation will presuppose some concepts. These two points indicate the need for the conviction in terms of the values inherent of the system, but do not remove the epistemological problem.

The Third Principle

The third principle states that there are knowledge claims that form part of the system that can only be known when one has achieved higher states of awareness. This principle places an important limitation on the first two. The system contains claims that one cannot verify in one's present sleeping state. Yet, at the same time, one should not believe such claims on the basis of faith.

To escape this dilemma, it is perhaps tempting to argue that we can have 'glimpses of the truth,' and argue that such glimpses give us a reason to believe the relevant aspects of the system. However, the problem with this suggestion becomes apparent when we ask 'Do such glimpses constitute knowledge? If they do, then the claim contradicts the third principle, which asserts that such knowledge is impossible in the sleeping state. If they do not constitute knowledge, then they cannot be used to justify other knowledge claims. In other words, the idea of glimpses does not alleviate the problem that the third epistemological principle places an important qualification or limitation on the first two.

The Fourth Principle

The fourth principle is that one can have higher indirect knowledge based on the direct experiences of others. The idea of indirect knowledge itself should not present us with special difficulties. Much of the ordinary knowledge we have is indirect. For example, most of us know indirectly that the moon is roughly 250,000 miles from the earth. This is indirect knowledge because we have not experienced this fact for ourselves. Nevertheless, this belief counts as knowledge for two reasons. First, some astronomers have more direct knowledge of the distance to the moon, having measured it. Second, we, who do not have this direct knowledge, have evidence that someone else knows it directly. For instance, we can justifiably assert that the scientists who claim to know this directly indeed do so. There is no reason to doubt them, and there are many other reasons for believing them.

However, the kind of 'higher' indirect knowledge claims asserted by Gurdjieff are more problematic than the example of the astronomers. In this case, the claim to knowledge depends on the state of consciousness of the person concerned. This implies that, in order for such indirect knowledge claims to be comparable to the example of the astronomers, it must satisfy two conditions. First, one must have some evidence to the effect that those people in the past were really were in higher states of consciousness, and second that, in such states of consciousness, one is able to know directly the metaphysical or cosmological claims in question.

Without satisfying these two conditions, the knowledge claims are in danger of being no more than appeals to authority or faith. As such, they contradict the first two epistemological principles referred to above.

The idea that such claims are appeals to authority leads us straight to a central aspect of Gurdjieff's system, namely the relationship between the teacher and his or her pupils. As we have seen, Gurdjieff claims that solitary work on oneself will not lead to results; it must be done in study groups, and such groups need a teacher who is not asleep. Furthermore, in order for such groups to function, its members need to have trust in the teacher. This general trust required for the work may *seem* to include the more specific trust that what the teacher says is true just because he knows that it is true.

At this point, it becomes important to separate the two kinds of values mentioned earlier. The claim 'Trust in the teacher is required for the work' attempts to justify trust by appeal to the values of self-development. It does not justify such trust by appeal to epistemological values, such as those expressed by the claim that one should only believe statements that have reasonable evidential backing. In order that this trust does not degenerate into faith, which is contrary to the first principle, it must not include the specific trust that what the teacher says is true because he or she knows it.

Conclusion

Can those aspects of Gurdjieff's system that do not fall under the first two epistemological principles nevertheless be counted as knowledge, even given that they are true? In summary, there seem to be only three possible answers to this question.

a) The first reply is that they can because if one were to achieve the results that the work aims for, then one would be able to verify those claims for oneself directly. This first reply depends on the notion of hypothetical verification.

b) The second reply is that they can constitute knowledge, but that they only count as indirect knowledge passed down by tradition. This reply depends on the two conditions mentioned above.

c) The third reply is that they cannot count as knowledge at all because of the first two epistemological principles, which imply that, in the case of statements that transcend ordinary knowledge, knowledge claims should be restricted to what we know directly through our own experience.

Please note that the epistemological problems discussed in this section are not specific to Gurdjieff's system. They apply to any body of putative knowledge that claims to transcend ordinary everyday knowledge and which is subject to the third principle mentioned above. For instance, similar points apply to many of the claims of the religions of the world and to some aspects of the metaphysics and epistemology of some metaphysical philosophers such as Spinoza.

More specifically, Spinoza claims that there is a state of intuition in which a person can immediately grasp the unity of everything.

However, the comparison to Spinoza requires a final important caution. Spinoza asserts that there is only one substance, the universe as a whole, which he calls God. This appears to be a metaphysical claim similar to some of Gurdjieff's affirmations and similar to some of the assertions made in Buddhist thought. However, from the epistemological point of view, this comparison between Gurdjieff and Spinoza is misleading because Spinoza offers arguments for his conclusion. This means that he does not consider that his main metaphysical claim is an empirical proposition to be confirmed or falsified by empirical observation. Rather, Spinoza considers it to be an a priori claim, which must be supported or defeated by a priori argument. In contrast, Gurdjieff's metaphysical claims appear to be empirical and, as such, they are subject to the epistemological conditions of empirical knowledge discussed here.

9
Science

In the previous chapter, we have seen that, even if Gurdjieff's claims are true, the idea that we can know that they are true requires defense, because knowledge is more than just true belief. Knowledge also requires reasonable evidence. In the previous chapter, we tried to reveal some of the problems inherent in such a defense. However, this does not address the objection that we do know that some of Gurdjieff's claims are false because they conflict with scientific knowledge. To assess this claim, we need to examine the relations between Gurdjieff's system and contemporary science. I shall restrict my comments to a few simple, but nevertheless contentious, points.

Evidence

It is important to separate two ideas. The first is that the scientific community does not acknowledge or recognize specific claims of the Gurdjieffian system. The second is that those claims actually contradict scientific knowledge. For example, it is one thing to claim that contemporary physicists have not found any evidence of finer forms of energy, which means that such propositions have no scientific evidence in favor of them. It is another thing to assert that such claims are actually contradicted by scientific knowledge, in which case there would be evidence that they are false. For example, if Gurdjieff's claim that there are finer levels of matter conflicts with the law of the conservation of energy, then there is a reason for disbelieving it.

This distinction is important because it means that rather than making a blanket opposition Gurdjieff's claims and those of science, an evaluation of his claims would require an identification of those specific aspects of his teaching that actually contradict well established scientific results.

The above distinction is important, but it is not so cut and dry. For example, in *Beelzebub,* Gurdjieff apparently claims that the earth has a second and smaller moon, Anulios. No such satellite has been observed. Of course, Gurdjieff's claim may be allegorical. If it is not then, the point is that such a satellite ought to be directly observable and the fact that it has not been detected, despite many different kinds of systematic observations of the solar system, counts as good evidence against its existence.

However, the above qualification only applies to those claims that should be directly observable. Thus, with regard to those that are not, we can insist on the original distinction between specific claims that are not recognized by the scientific community and those that actually contradict scientific knowledge.

The Limits of Science

In characterizing the relationship between Gurdjieff's system and science, it is easy to fall into the trap of making a dichotomy out of the two. Such a dichotomy arises in part by treating 'science' as if it were a monolithic institution with its own dogma and teaching, rather like a simplified portrait of the Catholic Church. For example, one might claim that science portrays the universe as a purely mechanical, purposeless physical system, and that, in contrast, Gurdjieff represents it as consisting of different levels of living beings each of which serves a purpose.

This dichotomy results in two opposite errors. On the one hand, we cannot validly argue in favor of Gurdjieff's ideas that the concepts of sciences are not sufficient to explain certain phenomena, such as consciousness or the existence of organic life and, therefore, certain Gurdjieffian claims are true. With such arguments, even if the premises are true, the conclusion does not follow. Such lines of thought presuppose a false dichotomy, namely that either 'science' or certain specific claims of Gurdjieff's system are correct.

On the other hand, we cannot argue against Gurdjieff's system merely on the grounds that it portrays the universe and human beings in ways that are radically different from the way the natural sciences do. We can see this by considering two questions.

1) Are the Natural Sciences Complete?

First, do the natural sciences give us a complete description of the universe? It seems pretty clear that they do not. Many of our ordinary everyday descriptions of the world are not part of and do not belong to the natural sciences. For example, the simple description of a person as angry can be true, but the concepts of person and anger have no place in physics, chemistry and biology. The same point applies to other psychological descriptions, to evaluative descriptions, such as 'This medicine will harm you' and more mundane statements, such as 'My cup is full.' This does not mean that such descriptions contradict science. Instead, it implies that the natural sciences do not offer a complete description of the world.

This indicates an important conclusion namely, that we should not conceive of the natural sciences as trying to give a general exclusive portrait of the universe at all. To do so is to confuse the specific empirical results of the natural sciences with a metaphysics based on certain scientific principles. For example, contemporary neurology does not claim that statements about consciousness can be reduced to sentences describing a neurological system. A scientific metaphysics might make such a claim, but the metaphysics has to be defended on philosophical grounds. Similarly, the theory of natural selection as such does not imply that the universe is purposeless, but a scientific metaphysics might. In this way, we do not have to conceive of the natural sciences as necessarily excluding other metaphysical views (Thomson, 2002).

2) Is the Scientific Method Complete?

Second, are the methodologies of the natural sciences the only way to gain knowledge of the world? This looks like a contentious question because many social scientists disagree radically about the use and place of the methodologies of the natural sciences within the social sciences. In what ways and to what extent should the social sciences employ the quantitative and experimental methods of the natural sciences? In some ways, this question has become an ideologically motivated debate.

A simple way to cut through this debate is to answer: it depends what kind of knowledge one wants and for what purposes one wants it. For example, we often have to rely on our understanding of the character traits of our friends and colleagues, but such knowledge is not scientific, because it does not depend on repeatable controlled experiments with quantifiable results. Knowledge requires reasonable evidence, but what counts as reasonable evidence depends to some extent on the context, nature and purpose of the knowledge claim involved. This does imply that it is entirely subjective, but rather that 'reasonable' is contextually sensitive. The danger is that this point may serve as an excuse for being lax. Nevertheless, knowledge is not exclusive to the scientific method. Consequently, the fact that

Gurdjieff's system is not scientific does not by itself constitute an argument against it.

In conclusion, we cannot argue in favor or against Gurdjieff's system simply in terms of a dichotomy between it and the natural sciences. Such lines of thought tend to degenerate into an ideological debate, which consists of a blanket opposition of science and mysticism, or of science and religion.

Language

In order for an empirical claim to be verifiable or falsifiable, it must have a relatively clear meaning. For example, the proposition that ordinary matter is animate is either obviously false or, it is not sufficiently clear to be verifiable or falsifiable. The word 'animate' has a perfectly normal meaning and, in general, we know what the criterial signs are for something being animate or alive. The moon does not show signs of being animate in this normal sense. For this reason, if someone claims that the moon is animate, then either he or she must be asserting something obviously false, or else proposing a conceptual revision or redefinition of 'animate.' In the latter case, to assess the proposed empirical claim, we need to know what the proposed criteria or revisions are. Otherwise, we do not know what the proposed empirical claim really means.

In affirming the above, I do not endorse a logical positivist theory of linguistic meaning. I am not asserting that the meaning of a sentence *is* its mode of verification or falsification. However, I am suggesting that an empirical claim should be clear enough to be in principle falsifiable before we can consider it true, because if no evidence can count against it, then no evidence can count in favor of it.

When asked whether anyone has reached a higher plane of being, Gurdjieff replied:

It means nothing if I say yes or no. If I say yes, you cannot verify it and if I say no, you are none the wiser. You have no business to believe me (Gurdjieff, 1975, p.78).

Gurdjieff recognizes that language has limitations. For example, he says that a language that has been constructed through our experience of unity and diversity in lower states of consciousness cannot express adequately the idea of unity available in the fourth state of consciousness (SM, p.279). In view of this, he uses allegories and analogies to express his ideas. This indicates recognition of the problem, but not a solution to it.

Concepts

There is a much more difficult question lurking in the background of this discussion, which is 'What warrants our use of a set of concepts?' The advance of science, and of knowledge generally, does not consist only in collecting facts or information. It also requires the development of new concepts or ways of classification with which we frame those facts.

However, the development of new concepts has to be warranted for example, by groups of observations and by their explanatory function. On the one hand, for example, the strange concepts of quantum mechanics are warranted by their capacity to explain and predict. On the other hand, the concepts of ether and phlogiston have become obsolete because they lacked explanatory and predictive power and were contradicted by various observations.

Similar points can be made about non-scientific concepts, such as 'person,' 'anger,' 'courage,' and 'poem.' Obviously such concepts make different kinds of classifications from, and serve very different kinds of interests compared to, scientific concepts, such as 'neutron' and 'mass.' Nevertheless, what warrants our use of them is their capacity to predict and explain within their own fields of operation. They effect classifications that serve the relevant interests.

This conclusion has two important implications. First, we cannot just assume that a set or family of concepts is legitimate. Second, Gurdjieff's central concepts, such as 'objective consciousness' and 'higher levels of being,' also must be warranted in terms of their capacity to explain and predict within their own fields of operation. This is the criterial sign of whether they make real classifications or not. This point leads us back to the discussion of the epistemological principles of the previous chapter.

Conclusion

In summary, we can create four boxes in which to put any empirical claim. This does not mean that we will know which box any specific claim should be placed.

1) Claims which are supported by the weight of evidence.

2) Those which are neither supported nor refuted by empirical evidence.

3) Claims which have the weight of empirical evidence against them.

4) Claims that are empirically unclear and cannot be placed in any of the first three boxes.

In the discussion of the last two chapters, I have tried to outline some of the principles of epistemology in order to indicate what an epistemological defense of Gurdjieff's system might look like. With a couple of exceptions, I have not tried to adjudicate which of his claims should go in which of the boxes.

In *Glimpses of the Truth,* Gurdjieff says:

> Judge everything from the point of view of your common sense. Become the possessor of your own sound ideas, and don't accept anything on faith; and when you, yourself, by way of sound reasoning and argument, come to an unshakable persuasion, to a full understanding of something, you will have achieved a certain degree of initiation (Gurdjieff, 1975, p.27).

General Concluding Remarks

I would like to conclude this book by returning to one of its central themes. This is the contrast between a paradox in Gurdjieff's system and its apparent solutions.

The paradox, mentioned by Ouspensky, arises from the fact that, beyond the preparatory stages, real progress requires the ability to work with the higher emotional center. Given this point, the paradox is 'How can a mechanical sleeping person lift him or herself above mechanicalness?' (Nicoll, 1954, p.67)

Within Gurdjieff's teaching, we find two different answers to this problem. First, there is the point that one needs to work with a teacher who is already awake. But, as Bennett notes, 'dependence upon highly trained and rarely equipped teachers is a serious defect for which it is difficult to see a remedy (Bennett, 1975, p. 246). The second solution is that there is 'a rope, above life' (Nicoll, 1954, p.67). In other words, as Ouspensky points out, a person already contains higher forms of energy. Given this, then there may be ways to work with or from these higher energies within. Picking up on the quote I have just cited from the *Glimpses of Truth,* these two answers become one if the teacher is within you.

10
Appendix 1:
A Meeting with a
Remarkable Man

Gurdjieff was born in 1866 in Alexandrapol, in Armenia. The date is disputed and uncertain (Moore, p.9 and p.339-40). His father, who came from a Greek Byzantine tradition, was a wealthy cattle owner who lost his fortune as the result of a cattle plague, and who became a carpenter (MRM, p.40). He was a bard with wide knowledge of central Asian folklore and myth. Gurdjieff's mother was Armenian. Gurdjieff had one brother and three sisters.

In 1877, the Russians decided to capture the area from the Turks. During this turbulent time of the Russio-Turkish war, the family moved to the Greek quarter of the city of Kars, where they stayed until 1885. The family lived in severe physical conditions.

At the time, Kars was a 'derelict frontier town' full of refugees from other parts of the region, such as Caucasians, Tartars, Assyrian Christians, Kurds, Gypsies, and Armenians (Bennett, 1973, p.16). The Turks brought a Sufi presence. There were strong Greek, Armenian and Russian Christian influences and the Yezidis had links back to the dualist Zoroastrian tradition. In his way, Gurdjieff was able to receive inspiration from all over central Asia within his hometown.

Kars was also a point of convergence of east and west. Because of his strong singing voice, Gurdjieff was admitted to the local choir. Dean Borsh of the Russian Orthodox Church gave the knowledge hungry Gurdjieff contact with Western culture and taught the boy astronomy, mathematics and chemistry (MRM p. 50). Gurdjieff also studied psychology, anatomy and physiology at the local military hospital. Gurdjieff read Greek, Armenian and Russian. Gurdjieff also participated in discussion groups on morality run by Deacon Bogachevsky, who became his moral guide (MRM, p.73-6 and Moore, p.16).

Around 1883, after his two mentors, Borsh and Bogachevsky, left Kars, Gurdjieff moved to Tiflis, the capital of Georgia (MRM, p.199-200). He lived with Pogossian, an old friend who was a student of Theology. During this period, Gurdjieff worked for the railway (MRM, p.86). In Tiflis, Gurdjieff met and became friends with Abram Yelov, a bookseller, who helped Gurdjieff find books describing traditions of the past (MRM p.110). During this period of his life, Gurdjieff felt

> An irrepressible striving to understand the precise significance, in general, of the life processes on earth (Gurdjieff, 1971, p.13).

Gurdjieff and Pogossian visited the ancient ruins of the ancient Armenian city of Ani and stumbled across parchments describing the Sarmoung Brotherhood of the 6th century located in Kurdistan (MRM, p. 87-90). Gurdjieff and Pogossian decided to find this ancient school.

The Searches

As a result, around the year 1887 until 1907, Gurdjieff traveled extensively in central Asia and visited North Africa and Europe. He was a member of an informal group of about 20 people, called the Seekers of Truth, which had the aim of studying ancient traditions and human psychology. During this period, described in *Meetings with Remarkable Men*, Gurdjieff lived through his own shrewd entrepreneurial activities, by working as a hypnotist and a healer, and perhaps by acting as a political agent. According to Bennett, Gurdjieff's period of search can be divided into four phases (Bennett, 1973, p.83 and 103). The dates of his voyages are very tentative.

1) In the first phase, from roughly 1887-1890, Gurdjieff tried to find explanations of the strange, apparently 'occult' phenomena that he

had seen in his childhood, such as the story of Yezidi, who could not leave a circle drawn around them (MRM, p. 66). Gurdjieff became convinced that such phenomena could not be explained adequately within existing scientific paradigms. In search of the Sarmoung school, he traveled with Pogossian into Turkey, south to Zakho, where they discovered a map of 'pre-sand Egypt' revealing ancient sites. As a result of this find, instead of heading to east to Kurdistan, they traveled west into Syria and to Alexandria in Egypt (MRM, p.106). After taking leave of Pogossian, Gurdjieff spent time in Jerusalem. In 1887, he worked in Egypt as a guide for tourists to the Sphinx and the Pyramid of Cheops and where he first met his friends, the Russian prince Yuri Lubovedsky, and Professor Skridlov. Possibly in 1888, Gurdjieff traveled from Thebes up the Nile with Prof. Skridlov. They spent three months in Abyssinia, where they learnt about the Coptic Church, and visited the Sudan. From there, he returned to the north, via Syria, and spent four months around the ruins of Babylon (MRM, p.225). In 1889, Gurdjieff may have spent time in Mecca and Medina trying to understand Islam (MRM, p.121). In 1890, he visited Constantinople and spent time with his friend Prince Lubovedsky (MRM, p.227).

2) During the second phase of Gurdjieff's search, from roughly 1891-98, he was trying to locate various ancient traditions of esoteric knowledge possessed by, among others, the Babylonians (Bennett, 1973, p.87). Possibly in 1893, Gurdjieff may have lived in Rome and visited Switzerland. In late 1895, Gurdjieff visited the monastery of Mount Athos, in Greece. In 1896, he was wounded and nearly killed in Crete (TS, p.7). After this, he was taken unconscious to the Holy Land, and from where he returned to the Caucasus, visiting Babylon again on the journey. Possibly in 1897, he visited Siberia, with Prof. Skridlov and Prince Yuri Lubovedsky in search of ancient knowledge (MRM, p.226).

3) During the third phase of his voyages, which began around 1898 and lasted until 1905, Gurdjieff apparently found evidence of the sources of ancient wisdom that he had been searching for. Probably in 1898, he and a group of 22 seekers traveled to central Asia, through northern Iran into the area around Sarmakand and Bokhara (MRM, p.183). Gurdjieff was living in Bokhara when he met Soloviev, an expert on Tibetan medicine (MRM, p.135). It was perhaps around that time that he and Soloviev were able to find, east of Bokhara, the main source of the knowledge that he had been looking for, namely the monastery of the Sarmoung, where they met coincidentally Gurdjieff's friend Prince Lubovedsky (MRM, p.161; SM, p.36).

In 1899, Gurdjieff spent time in a Sufi monastery in northern Afghanistan (Bennett, 1973, p.92). In 1900, Gurdjieff was part of an expedition through the Hindu Kush to northern India (MRM, p. 209). Around 1901, he arrived in Tibet, where he studied Buddhism until 1904. In Tibet, he was injured a second time by a stray bullet and, as a result of his closeness to death, he had a mystical experience in the oasis of Yangi Hissar on the edge of the Gobi desert (TS, p.9-25). As a result of this, he took an oath to use his charisma and hypnotic abilities only for good purposes (TS, p.16).

In 1904, he returned to his family in Alexandropol. Late that year, he set out again on his travels and, shortly afterwards, he was shot a third time (TS, p.9). After this incident, Gurdjieff revisited Yangi Hissar, in Chinese Turkestan, on the southwestern edge of the Gobi desert, where he recuperated.

4) The fourth phase of his search began in 1905, when he moved to the area around Tashkent, where he stayed, possibly for two years, in a Yesivi dervish monastery nearby, learning various sacred dances, music and rhythmic exercises (Gurdjieff, 1971, p.19-20; Bennett, 1973, p.105). Finally, he settled in Tashkent.

First Contacts

In 1908, having found the teachings and techniques he had been searching for, Gurdjieff started to put them into practice in the city of Tashkent. He worked as a professional hypnotist. He formulated the aim to 'help people to attain inward freedom' and planned to disseminate this understanding in the West. During this period, Gurdjieff was probably in contact with a spiritual group or monastery in the region of Kashgaria (Gurdjieff, 1971, p.59; Bennett, 1973, p.111).

In 1910, he set up shop as a spiritual teacher in Tashkent. He started to form study or work groups. He also started various money making ventures, including trading in carpets (MRM, 270). Gurdjieff found that he could not devote enough time to his work groups and, therefore, he decided to set up an institute to train others to help him with his mission in the West. In 1911, Gurdjieff made his second oath. He vowed to lead 'an artificial life' for 21 years, according to a pre-planned program, which conflicted with his own character-traits (Gurdjieff, 1971, p.11-2).

As a consequence of his decisions, in 1912, he moved to Moscow and established the Institute for the Harmonious Development of Man (Bennett, 1973, p.116). He began to lecture and teach dances in

Moscow and later in St. Petersburg, attracting the attention of intellectual society. Gurdjieff was friendly with the Russian aristocrats and had contact with the Russian royal family. He feel in love with and married a lady in waiting to the Tsarina, called Countess Julia Ostrowska, who became the central figure in his dance, the Initiation of the Priestess (Moore, p.67).

He gathered around him a group, which included Vladimir Pohl, director of the Russian Musical Society; the famous sculptor, Sergio Mercourov; his first foreign student, the pianist Sir Paul Dukes; and Dr. Leonid Stjoernval, who stayed with Gurdjieff until 1932 (Moore, p.71-7).

Meanwhile, Russia was in the middle of a war and internal collapse. Gurdjieff was producing a ballet called *The Struggle of the Magicians*, which attracted the attention of the author of *Tertium Organum*, Peter Ouspensky. In April 1915, Gurdjieff met Ouspensky, who later became one of his most valued pupils. Ouspensky established groups in St. Petersburg, then called Petrograd, and frequently traveled to Moscow to be with Gurdjieff. They were in contact for four years, and Ouspensky's reports of what Gurdjieff taught him those years, primarily contained in the two books, *In Search of the Miraculous* and *The Fourth Way*, may be considered as definitive statements of Gurdjieff's teaching of the time. However, the first report of Gurdjieff's teaching was *Glimpses of the Truth*, written anonymously by one of his pupils in the winter of 1914-5 (Gurdjieff, 1975, p.3-41). Between February and August 1916, Gurdjieff taught his whole system to the St. Petersburg group.

In 1917, Thomas de Hartman and his aristocratic wife Olga became Gurdjieff's pupils. Hartman was a well-known composer of the time. He was later to arrange and play Gurdjieff's piano music. Olga became Gurdjieff's indefatigable secretary or assistant.

As revolution threatened St. Petersburg, Gurdjieff left for Alexandrapol to visit his family. 'When Gurdjieff and Mme Ostrowska boarded the train, the Tsar still reigned, and when they got off he did not' (Moore, p.97). In July 1917, Gurdjieff settled in Essentuki in the south. He gathered 12 of his students to work intensively for six weeks on various exercises. This was probably to try out some of the techniques he intended to use for his Institute (Bennett, 1973, p.120). Ouspensky describes the work of this period (SM, p.346). When Gurdjieff suddenly announced that he was breaking up the study group, Ouspensky began to feel a separation between him and the person of Gurdjieff (SM, p.373). Later, Ouspensky formed his own groups, spreading Gurdjieff's teaching in Istanbul and in London, from 1922 until his death in 1947. Although Ouspensky never totally lost contact with Gurdjieff and visited him a few times, this was the beginning of a permanent split.

In March 1918, Gurdjieff moved to Tuapse, on the Black Sea, where he and a group of ten students, including the Hartmanns, lived for two months. Given the political instability of the region, Gurdjieff decided to move on across the Caucasus Mountains to the relative safety of Sochi. He summoned his family from Alexandrapol, and he invited his Moscow and Petrograd students to his temporary base in Essentuki. In July 1918, Gurdjieff's family arrived, although his father stayed at the family home and was killed by the invading Turks (Moore, p.117 and MRM, p.45).

In August 1918, after careful planning and work to obtain the required official permissions, Gurdjieff and a group of 21 students undertook a hazardous expedition to a remote area of the Caucasus mountains, ostensibly for a geological survey, but in reality to escape the war by moving to Sochi. Gurdjieff describes this arduous trek over the mountains in *Meetings with Remarkable Men* (MRM, p.272-6). Thomas Hartman also tells the story in *Our Life with Mr. Gurdjieff.*

However, Sochi was only temporarily safe. In January 1919, Gurdjieff, his wife and the de Hartmanns and the Stjoernvals moved to Tiflis, now called Tbilisi. The situation in Tbilisi was calm and Gurdjieff sent for his family and his pupils. Suddenly, he was responsible for a large group of people, and he started a carpet business that quickly flourished. De Hartmann became Professor of composition at the Conservatoire of Advanced Musical Studies, and his wife sung in Carmen at the Opera House. Around Easter 1919, two important pupils, Alexander de Salzmann, an artist, and his wife, Jeanne, a professional dancer, joined the group. Jeanne Salzmann, who later effectively became Gurdjieff's deputy, organized the first public performance of Gurdjieff's movements in the Opera House in June 1919. Gurdjieff established his Institute for the Harmonious Development of Man in Tbilisi. He attracted new students, including the talented dancer Olgivanna, who later married the famous architect Frank Lloyd Wright (Moore, p.133). Gurdjieff began preparing the ballet, *The Struggle of the Magicians*, which, in the event, was never publicly performed. At this time, Tbilisi was under British control. However, the British planned to withdraw their army and support of the Menshevik Government. Following the warnings of Major Pinder, later a Gurdjieff pupil, Gurdjieff decided to move further west, to Turkey,

Despite being regarded as a suspicious character and possibly a communist spy, in June 1920, Gurdjieff moved to Istanbul, with 30 members of his group. Gurdjieff settled in quickly and once again started to organize his planned institute with the help of Ouspensky, who had independently moved to Istanbul and with whom there was a temporary reconciliation. De Hartmann started to establish a new orchestra in Istanbul and began collaborating with Gurdjieff on musical compositions. It was at this time that John Bennett, who was working for British military intelligence in Turkey, was introduced to Gurdjieff. Bennett was to become a student of Ouspensky's in London, an exponent of Gurdjieff's ideas and a founder of his own school in England. In August 1921, Ouspensky moved to London where his new book had attracted the attention of some wealthy people, including Lady Rothermere, wife of the newspaper owner. Mme Sophie Ouspensky, however, decided to remain as one of Gurdjieff's pupils (Moore, p.153).

Ultimately, Gurdjieff wanted to move to Western Europe to establish his institute (MRM, p.282). He had received an invitation to teach his movements and dances in Dresden, Germany. In August 1921, he and some of his pupils traveled through Eastern Europe to Germany. In the event, nothing materialized for Gurdjieff in Germany. For a while, he had the idea of settling in England, which he visited twice and where he gained the allegiance of some of Ouspensky's pupils, including, Dr. Maurice Nicoll, a Jungian psychiatrist and Alfred Orage, the editor of the *New Age*. As a result, the break between Gurdjieff and Ouspensky became public. In July 1922, Gurdjieff moved to Paris (MRM, p.285; Moore, p.167).

Fontainebleau

He was, however, in great financial difficulties. He sought to earn money in Paris from curing drunkards and drug addicts, and he started various business ventures. Meanwhile, with the help of Olga de Hartmann, in October 1922, Gurdjieff managed to acquire a castle called the Château du Prieuré, near Fontainbleau, about 40 miles from Paris.

Now began what Gurdjieff calls 'one of the maddest periods of my life' (MRM, p.285). New students began to arrive at the Prieuré, including Maurice Nicoll and Orage. Gurdjieff pushed his students to complete the renovation of the Prieuré in three months, while he worked on his business ventures during the daytime in Paris, tending to their needs during the evenings and long nights. The group worked frantically. One person described the subsequent physical and mental exhaustion as greater than that produced by 'the winter trenches in Flanders 1917' (Moore, p.178). It was at this time that Katherine Mansfield, the New Zealand novelist, arrived at the Prieuré, with advanced tuberculosis. She died at the Prieuré in January 1923, generating unwanted publicity for the group. Ouspensky briefly visited the Prieuré in September 1923.

Once the work on the renovation was completed, Gurdjieff acquired an aircraft hangar from which the group constructed a study house, where his students could perform the dances. It was a huge area draped with oriental carpets, with a bank of seats and divans (Bennett, 1973, p.140 and Moore, p.182). At the end of 1923, Gurdjieff's dances were performed in Paris, at the Theatre of the Champs Elysées. During this period, Gurdjieff's mother and sister arrived in France. Fritz Peters, who was child at the time, later vividly described this hectic life at the Prieuré in his book, *Boyhood with Gurdjieff* (see also, Moore, Chapters 8 and 9). Peter Brooke's film of Gurdjieff's book, *Meeting with Remarkable Men* concludes with a sequence of Gurdjieffian dances.

In January 1924, Gurdjieff and his troupe went to the USA for the first time, to promote his teaching and to perform the movements and exercises on the East Coast. He acquired new pupils including the writer Jean Toomer, Jane Heap and Margaret Anderson, the editors of the avant-garde *Little Review*. The final New York performance was held in Carnegie Hall in March, after which there was a brief visit to Chicago. Gurdjieff returned to Paris in June 1924 with a group of new American pupils.

The Writer

In July 1924, Gurdjieff crashed his car into a tree near the Fontainbleau Forest. He nearly died. After some time at the hospital, he was brought to the Prieuré unconscious. His mother, sister and wife nursed him. Olga de Hartmann and Ouspensky's wife, Sophie, ran the Prieuré, which was supported financially by the Gurdjieff groups established in the USA by Orage.

The accident effectively meant the end of the Prieuré as a school. As Gurdjieff recovered, he changed his plans. He decided to write and, in August, to the great consternation of his pupils, he closed the Prieuré as a school. Some of his students left (Moore, p.209). By the fall of 1924, Gurdjieff could move about the house and, towards the end of the year, he began to dictate to Olga de Hartmann (Gurdjieff, 1971, p.42).

After some writing experiments, Gurdjieff decided to write three works. The first would be aimed to destroy people's false beliefs about reality and themselves; the second would show that there are other ways of thinking and other types of value; the third would show how to encounter reality (Gurdjieff, 1971, p.47). These works are *Beelzebub's Tales to his Grandson, Meetings with Remarkable Men*, and *Life is only Real then: When 'I Am.'* The series as a whole is called *All and Everything*.

In June 1925, Gurdjieff's mother died and, by then, his wife had contracted cancer. When not working on his book, Gurdjieff dedicated himself to his wife's care. In June 1926, she died. During the period from July 1925 to May 1927, while writing *Beelzebub*, Gurdjieff composed music with Thomas de Hartmann (Moore, p.214). They wrote over 100 short pieces, several of which were preludes to the reading of particular chapters of the book.

When Gurdjieff started writing, people began to visit the Prieuré again. By 1926, it was full of life. However, there was no formal teaching, or organized work, nor movements and exercises. Gurdjieff was usually inaccessible to the visitors, although he gave personal attention to many people. He preferred to write away from the Prieuré, usually in cafés. The Grand Café in Paris was referred to as his Paris office. Sometimes, he would invite visitors on hair-raising car trips (Bennett, 1973, p.168).

Drafts of the first book, *Beelzebub's Tales to his Grandson*, were read to the visitors and pupils. There were even public readings of the book. By 1927, he was hoping to publish the work the following year. However, people not connected to Gurdjieff were not able to understand his work. In November 1927, after entering into a suicidal depression, and despite the frail condition of his body, he decided to rewrite the whole work, He decided that his literary output required conscious suffering on his own part (TS, p.32-5). Later, he also decided to 'press the most sensitive corn of everyone he met' (TS, p.44).

In May 1928, he realized the exact form that his own conscious intentional suffering should take. He decided that he needed to send his closest pupils and friends away from the Prieuré, although this does not mean that he lost contact with them altogether (TS, p.45). One by one, they went. Soon after, Margaret Anderson stopped visiting the Institute. In 1928, Mme Sophie Ouspensky was dispatched to London to revitalize the groups there. Alexander and Jeanne Salzman, who had joined Gurdjieff in 1918, were sent to Germany (although Jeanne later returned to the Prieuré). On his second trip to New York in January 1929, he urged Thomas and Olga de Hartmann to start an independent life, which they did that summer, although the final parting with Olga was not until the spring of 1930. Fritz Peters left the Prieuré in September 1929. Furthermore, on his next two trips to the USA, Gurdjieff apparently tried to alienate his American followers by publicly denouncing Orage, who was at the time in London. In December 1930, he asked the American pupils to sign an oath severing relations with Orage, an oath that Orage himself signed (TS, p.100). Lastly, in 1931, he had a final argument with Ouspensky, who wanted to visit the Prieuré (Bennett, 1973, p.235; Moore, p.238-40).

Apparently, Gurdjieff undertook these drastic changes to complete his writing mission. By the summer of 1931, only two of his original pupils remained in the Prieuré, Jeanne Salzmann and Leonid Stjoernval. However, by the autumn of 1928, he had completed the recasting of *Beelzebub* and he started work on the second book in the series, *Meetings with Remarkable Men*. He still attracted new pupils, including the American writer Katherine Hulme. However, his financial situation was desperate and, in May 1932, the Prieuré had to be sold (Moore p.246). Stjoernval and Jeanne Salzmann went to live elsewhere and Gurdjieff moved to Paris to live on his own.

After finishing *Meetings with Remarkable Men*, Gurdjieff started to plan the third book in the series. On the 13th September 1932, he hurriedly wrote a pamphlet called *The Herald of Coming Good,* which he later advised people not to read (TS, p.50). His sixth visit to the US was a disaster. Toomer wrote that Gurdjieff 'seemed to be tearing down everything he created' (Moore, p.248).

Despite this, in the fall of 1932, Gurdjieff left on his own for a prolonged stay in the US, where he met Frank Lloyd Wright for the first time in June 1934. Things seemed to start to pick up. In November, he started writing his third book, the prologue of which was finished in April. Also, in April 1935, the news reached him in New York that the Prieuré was up for sale, and that the wealthy US Senator Cutting might be willing to finance his work and even the purchase of the Prieuré. However, in May, the Senator was killed when his plane exploded on his way to meet Gurdjieff. Afterwards, Gurdjieff vanished.

New Phase: Teaching

In October 1935, Gurdjieff suddenly reappeared in Paris, where he lived in various apartments, until he settled in 6 Rue des Colonels Rénard, where he remained for 13 years. In October 1935, he formed his first Parisian group, which included Jane Heap, Kathryn Hulme and Solita Solano, a writer who became his secretary in 1937. One of his later work groups consisted exclusively in lesbian pupils. From July 1936, Gurdjieff reestablished contact with Jeanne Salzmann, who was 'emerging as Gurdjieff's de facto deputy' (Moore, p.268). During this period until his death, Gurdjieff seems to have been more settled and conciliatory. He often cooked for his pupils. He resumed his frequent car trips around Europe. When he visited the US in March 1939, his students there urged him to remain for the duration of the war that now threatened Europe. Instead, he returned to Paris, where he stocked up his pantry with provisions. During the German occupation, he gathered around him a 'big family,' a group of people whom he helped in these times of deprivation through his black-market dealings (Moore, p.276). Meanwhile, his French group was growing in numbers.

After the European war finished in May 1945, his students from England began to visit him again. He welcomed them, 'Do not be afraid any more. You are at home here. I am your new father' (Moore, p.289). Furthermore, when Ouspensky died in October 1947, his wife, Sophie, who was now in New Jersey, advised Ouspensky's pupils to visit Gurdjieff. John Bennett also returned to Gurdjieff with his own pupils. In the midst of this activity, in August 1948, Gurdjieff had another car accident (Moore, p.295). In the winter of 1948, in the US, he met, for the last time, Mme. Sophie Ouspensky, who gave Gurdjieff a copy of her husband's manuscript, *In Search of the Miraculous*. Gurdjieff approved the publication of the book. By now, Gurdjieff was suffering from physical pain. In October 1949, he collapsed in one of his Movements classes. Later that month, he received the proof copy of *Beelzebub*. On the 29th October 1949, he died.

A few months before his death, Gurdjieff had signaled to Bennett that a new teacher would come from the Dutch East Indies and, consequently, Bennett later joined the spiritual movement, Subud, originating from Indonesia (Bennett, 1975, p.257). Although many Gurdjieff groups exist around the world each with their own teachers, Jeanne Salzmann in effect became the leader of the Gurdjieff movement until her death in 1990.

The Person

What kind of person was Gurdjieff? This question is surrounded by controversy. Many writers on Gurdjieff claim that he was an extraordinary person with supernatural powers. On the other hand, his detractors claim that he was a charlatan, who exercised tremendous personal power in a disrespectful way over some of his students.

Looking over his life as a whole, some conclusions seem clear. First, he was obviously a person of tremendous strength, energy and courage. For example, he arrived in Europe, without any knowledge of European languages, with many people to support. Second, he was clearly a very generous person, who dedicated his life to teaching and to the development of his students, many of whom he supported financially. Third, he was person with a great sense of humor who mercilessly teased his pupils. Fourth, he had an extraordinary range of talents. For example, he started many businesses that flourished. In addition to his dances, music and writing, he was an excellent cook and had many practical skills, in areas such as carpentry and construction.

Fifth, he had a complex relationship with truth. On the one hand, he spent his life trying to discover and impart 'truths' of many kinds. On the other, perhaps because of his decisions of 1911 and May 1928, Gurdjieff projected many different personalities or personas, which makes it difficult to recognize the real person. Additionally, consider his work *Beelzebub*. On the one hand, Gurdjieff wanted it to available to the general public. On the other, he deliberately sought to disguise some elements of his teaching through the use of analogy and symbolism so that readers would have to struggle with the work.

Sixth, Gurdjieff had an extremely forceful charisma and he evoked strong reactions in those around him. Given this point, deeper understanding of the man becomes problematic because it is very difficult to perceive Gurdjieff himself by seeing how the people close to him saw him. It is hard to see him by the light of their reflections of him, because their reactions vary and are so strong. In the words of the author Henry Miller, Gurdjieff could be

> tender, fierce, strict, indulgent, wise, clownish, utterly serious and a *farceur* all at one time (F. Peters, 1980, p.1).

Why has the character of Gurdjieff attracted so much attention? Beyond sensationalism and curiosity, there are two reasons. First, the pupil-teacher relationship is a central feature of his teachings. Such a relationship requires trust and, in this way, the question arises: In what ways could he be trusted as a teacher? However, in part, this question is beside the point. We cannot discredit or vindicate his teaching and its practical applications by trying to discredit or vindicate him.

Second, the life and character of Gurdjieff challenge most preconceptions of what a spiritual person and teacher should be. Gurdjieff is not like our traditional conception of a saint or spiritual leader. However, Gurdjieff once said:

> I am the signpost. I indicate a way. But you do not follow a signpost; you follow the road. You are not to follow me; you are to practice the method I define (Webb, p.551).

Given this, perhaps, the whole idea that certain persons constitute a general model of what a spiritual person should be like is mistaken.

11
Appendix 2
Glossary

Some Vocabulary in 'Beelzebub'

Triamazikamno: the law of three.

Heptaparaparshinokh: the law of seven.

Autoegocratic-process: the process of self-maintenance by which the Endlessness or Source generates the Sun Absolute.

Trogoautoegocratic-process: reciprocal maintenance.

Theomertmalogos: the Word-God, the primary emanation from the Sun Absolute.

Kundabuffer: the organ that originally made humans in a state of sleep.

Etherokrilno: the primary formless material of the universe (Bel. p.137).

Handledzoin: the energy or substance of the higher body of humans; higher emotional energy.

Omnipresent Okidanokh: the omnipresent active element; the fundamental cause of all cosmic phenomena (Bel, p.138-9).

Djartklom: the process by which the Okidanokh separates into three forces (Bel, p140).

Vivifyingness of Vibrations: the degree of vibration in cosmic scale of vibrations.

Iraniranumange: the process of the common cosmic exchange of energies or substances (Bel p.759 & 762).

Partkdolgduty: conscious labor and intentional suffering.

Our Common Father Endlessness: the source of everything (World 1).

Heropass: Time.

Harnelmiatznel: the process whereby a finer energy arises out of a coarser one.

Harnel-Aoot: the fifth stopbinder (Bel, 754).

12
Bibliography

Anderson, Margaret, *The Unknowable Gurdjieff*, Routledge, 1975

Bennett, J.G, *Gurdjieff: Making a New World*, Turnstone, 1973

Bennett, J.G., *Witness*, Turnstone Books, 1975

Bennett, J.G, *Talks on Beelzebub's Tales*, Samuel Weiser, 1988

Bennett, J.G., *The Dramatic Universe, Volume 1*, Hodder and Stoughton, 1956

Bennett, J.G., *The Dramatic Universe, Volume 2*, Hodder and Stoughton, 1961

Bennett, J.G., *A Spiritual Psychology*, Coombe Springs Press, 1964

Gurdjieff, G.I, *Views from the Real World*, Dutton, 1975

Gurdjieff, G.I., *Beelzebub's Tales to His Grandson*, Dutton, 1964

Gurdjieff, G.I., *Meetings with Remarkable Men*, Routledge, 1963

Gurdjieff, G.I., *Life is Real Only Then, When 'I Am,'* Viking, 1991

Gurdjieff, G.I., *The Herald of Coming Good*, Weiser, 1971

Hartman, Thomas and Olga, *Our Life with Mr. Gurdjieff*,

Moore, James, *Gurdjieff: The Anatomy of a Myth*, Element Books, 1991

Nicoll, Maurice, *The New Man*, Hermitage House, 1951

Nicoll, Maurice, *Psychological Commentaries on the Teaching of Gurdjieff and Ouspensky*, Vols, 1-5, Stuart and Watkins, 1960-4

Nicoll, Maurice, *The Mark*, Vincent Stuart, 1954

Ouspensky, P.D., *In Search of the Miraculous*, Routledge, 1969

Ouspensky, P.D., *The Fourth Way*, Routledge, 1972

Peters, F, *Boyhood with Gurdjieff,* Capra Press, 1980
Thomson, Garrett, *On Kant,* Wadsworth, 2000
Thomson, Garrett, *On the Meaning of Life*, Wadsworth, 2002
Webb, James, *The Harmonious Circle*, Putnam's Sons, 1980